CULTURES OF THE WORLD
VENEZUELA

Jane Kohen Winter/Kitt Baguley

BENCHMARK BOOKS

MARSHALL CAVENDISH
NEW YORK

PICTURE CREDITS
Cover photo: © Trip/P. Musson
Chicago White Sox: 108 (both) • Mario Corvetto/Evergreen Photo Alliance:
106 • DDB Stock Photo: 5, 86 • Victor Englebert: 19, 28, 29, 30, 35, 43, 56,
57 (bottom), 60, 63 (top), 74, 101, 104 (top) • Getty Images/Hulton Archive:
31 • Eduardo Gil: 6, 51, 53, 68, 112, 122, 130 • Rankin Harvey/Houserstock:
47 • HBL Network Photo Agency: 45, 46 • Dave G. Houser/Houserstock: 42
• The Hutchison Library: 4, 9, 59 (top), 91 • Lonely Planet: 18 • Chip &
Rosa Maria Peterson: 3, 7, 8 (bottom), 11, 13 (both), 16, 36, 37 (top), 39, 52,
54, 59 (bottom), 62, 63 (bottom), 64, 67, 71, 80, 81, 85, 103, 113, 115, 117,
121, 126 • South American Pictures: 1, 8 (top), 10, 12, 14, 17, 20, 21, 22, 24,
26, 27, 32, 34, 37 (bottom), 38, 40, 50, 55, 57 (top), 58, 66, 72, 73, 77, 79, 82,
87, 89, 90, 93, 94, 95, 96, 97, 98, 100, 102, 104 (bottom), 105, 107, 111, 124,
128, 129 • Times Media Private Limited: 131 • Topham Picturepoint: 49
• Trip Photographic Library: 76 • Venezuelan Consulate of Chicago: 23, 114

ACKNOWLEDGMENTS
With thanks to Jennifer Vickers of East Carolina University,
for her expert reading of the manuscript.

PRECEDING PAGE
Boys from the Orinoco Delta.

Marshall Cavendish Corporation
99 White Plains Road
Tarrytown, NY 10591
Website: www.marshallcavendish.com

© 1990, 2002 by Times Media Private Limited
All rights reserved. First edition 1990.
Second edition 2002.

Originated and designed by
Times Books International, an imprint of
Times Media Private Limited, a member of the
Times Publishing Group

Printed in Malaysia

Library of Congress Cataloging-in-Publication Data:
Winter, Jane Kohen, [date]
    Venezuela / Jane Kohen Winter, Kitt Baguley—2nd ed.
        p. cm.—(Cultures of the world)
    Includes bibliographical references and index.
    Summary: Presents the geography, history, government, economy,
and social life and customs of the South American country of Venezuela.
    ISBN 0-7614-1362-6
    1. Venezuela—Juvenile literature. [1. Venezuela.] I. Baguley, Kitt. II. Title. III. Series

6 5 4 3 2 1

CONTENTS

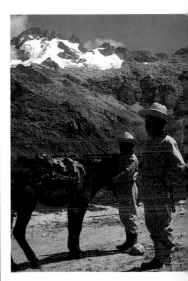

Venezuelan children of the Andes with their mules, near Pico Bolívar, the country's tallest peak.

3

**A Venezuelan girl of
African origin.**

4

INTRODUCTION

VENEZUELA IS A LAND of superlatives. It is the wealthiest nation in South America, thanks to its petroleum reserves. It has some of the world's oldest, most mysterious geologic formations, the world's highest waterfall, and some of the world's rarest, most unusual flowers and animals.

Superlatives apply equally to the people of Venezuela. *Caraqueños* ("kah-rah-KAIR-nyohs"), citizens of the capital city, Caracas, are some of the most sophisticated South Americans. Simón Bolívar, one of South America's most revered heroes, who led several South American nations on the road to independence, was born in Caracas. The Venezuelan population also includes some of the toughest, most hardworking South Americans, the *llaneros* ("yah-NAIR-rohs"), cowboys of the grasslands. Every year, the *llaneros* battle extremely inhospitable weather—floods in the wet season and drought in the dry season—to feed their cattle.

Cultures of the World: Venezuela explores the history, economy, environment, people, faiths, festivals, food, and lifestyles of this remarkable country in South America.

GEOGRAPHY

THE SEVENTH LARGEST COUNTRY in South America, Venezuela lies in the north of the continent. With a total area of 352,144 square miles (912,050 square km), Venezuela is slightly more than twice the size of California, about four times the size of Great Britain, around 28 times the size of Holland, yet only one-tenth the size of Brazil.

Venezuela's coastline stretches 2,800 miles (4,506 km) and abuts both the Caribbean Sea and the Atlantic Ocean. Half of the country is covered by forests and beaches; the other half consists of mountains, plains, deserts, and grasslands. Venezuelan land can be divided into four distinct geographical regions: the Andean Highlands, the Maraicaibo basin, the *llanos*, and the Guiana Highlands.

THE ANDEAN HIGHLANDS

The Andean Highlands lie in the west and along the coast. They include the Andean mountain range within the Venezuelan border. Though these highlands represent only 12 percent of Venezuela's land area, they are home to 66 percent of the national population and most of the major cities. The capital, Caracas, is in this region. With its pleasant climate, Caracas has been called "Los Angeles without the smog." It is one of the world's most sophisticated cities, with a skyline of high-rise office and apartment buildings and a modern French-designed subway system. Yet the capital is as poor as it is wealthy: thousands of *caraqueños* live in *ranchos* ("RAHN-chohs"), or makeshift shacks, on the fringes of the city.

Opposite: **The Caribbean coast of northern Venezuela.**

Below: **Pico Bolívar, the tallest peak in Venezuela, just before sunset.**

7

"...a wide and stretching land, all horizons like hope, all roads like the will."

—*Rómulo Gallegos, describing the* llanos *in his novel,* Doña Bárbara

The *llanos* of Venezuela.

A single spark in the scorching heat of the dry season can cause extensive damage to the *llanos*.

THE MARACAIBO BASIN

The second major geographical region, the Maracaibo basin, lies in the northwest of the country. This area contains Lake Maracaibo, the largest lake in South America. This shallow freshwater lake is 75 miles (121 km) long and 100 miles (161 km) wide. At the northern tip, where the lake opens into the Caribbean Sea, lies the port of Maracaibo. In the early part of the 20th century, the most important oil wells in Venezuela were discovered in Lake Maracaibo. Now, the lake is dotted with thousands of oil derricks that extract millions of barrels of oil each year. With a population of almost two million, the city of Maracaibo is the second largest city in Venezuela. It is accessible via the five-mile-long (8-km-long) General Raphael Urdaneta Bridge, the longest prestressed concrete bridge in the world.

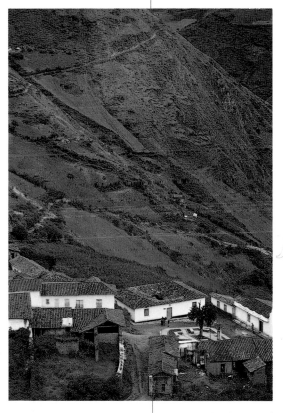

Los Nevados is one of the highest villages in Venezuela. Vegetation here is more interesting than on the *llanos*, and conditions are more hospitable for human settlement.

THE LLANOS

The *llanos* ("YAH-noss"), or plains, are located in the central part of the country. They account for nearly one-third of Venezuelan land, yet they are home to only 9 percent of the population. This low population density is due to the extremely harsh landscape and climate. The land is flat and almost treeless, and the seasons range from scorching hot to soaking wet. Five million head of cattle live in the *llanos*. The herds are driven by the cowboys, or *llaneros*, to wetter areas during the dry season and to drier areas during the wet season.

THE GUIANA HIGHLANDS

Located in the south and east of Venezuela, the Guiana Highlands account for almost half the nation's land, yet are almost completely uninhabited. These highlands consist mainly of ancient, vast sandstone formations called *tepuis* ("teh-POO-ees"), or tablelands. The *tepuis* can reach as high as 6,000 feet (1,829 m) and have been eroded at the base. Since many of the *tepuis* in this region are very steep and virtually unscalable, much of the Guiana Highlands remain unexplored.

A cloud-topped *tepui*.

The Guiana Highlands also contain the world's highest waterfall, Angel Falls, first spotted by pilot James Angel in 1935 while he was searching for gold. At 3,212 feet (979 m), the falls are more than 15 times taller than Niagara Falls, or twice the height of New York's Empire State Building. Strangely enough, Angel Falls does not flow over a cliff. The water actually accumulates underground and erupts through cracks in the mountain.

The largest city in the Guiana Highlands is Ciudad Guayana, with 603,000 inhabitants. Guayana is also the fifth largest city in Venezuela and a hub for heavy industry.

THE ISLANDS

Venezuelan territory includes 72 islands in the Caribbean Sea. The most popular of these, Margarita Island, known for its beaches and colonial architecture, is a favorite resort for Venezuelans and tourists.

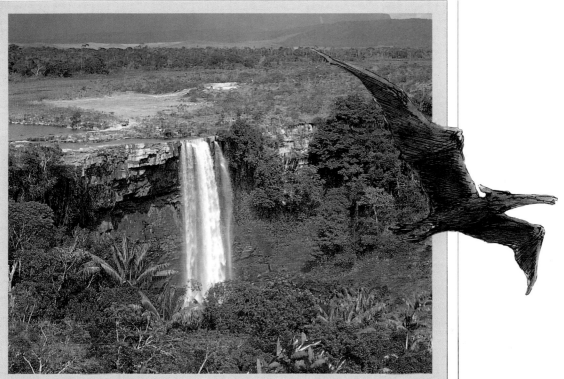

THE LOST WORLD

The Guiana Highlands have been used as a setting in a famous piece of literature. Sir Arthur Conan Doyle's *The Lost World*, originally published in 1912, is a fantasy-adventure tale about an expedition by four English adventurers to a remote region in Venezuela, where 20-foot pterodactyls, gigantic three-toed, black-skinned dinosaurs, and apemen still roamed.

Prehistoric creatures do not, of course, exist in the Guiana Highlands. But the Guiana Highlands have in fact been a largely unexplored place, due to the unfriendly terrain.

"It's the grandest, richest, most wonderful bit of earth upon this planet. …Why shouldn't somethin' new and wonderful lie in such a country? And why shouldn't we be the men to find out?" asks a character from *The Lost World*. Modern scientists and explorers are perhaps asking themselves the same question. Apart from scattered groups of Indians, no one inhabits the Guiana Highlands. However, industry is finding its way into the region to exploit bauxite, iron ore, and gold deposits and to generate hydroelectric power by damming some rivers near Ciudad Guayana.

THE GREAT ORINOCO

Columbus was the first known explorer to see the mouth of the Orinoco River. This river, with its 436 tributaries, is the third longest river in South America and the eighth longest in the world. It flows 1,370 miles (2,205 km) from the Guiana Highlands to the Atlantic Ocean. On the way, the Orinoco splits into 100 separate channels, and at the end of the journey, the channels rush into the Atlantic Ocean with such great force that there is fresh water for miles out to sea.

At one point, the Orinoco River connects with the great Amazon River through a waterway called the Casiquiare Canal. It is said that together the Orinoco and the Amazon form the greatest river system in the world. They carry more water and drain a larger area than both the Missouri-Mississippi system and the Nile.

In fact, more than a third of South America—an area of approximately 2.5 million square miles (6.5 million square km)—is dominated by the Orinoco-Amazon river system. The Orinoco also provides important communication links with the interior of Venezuela and hydroelectric power for a large part of the country.

Above right: **The tropical rain forest of the Orinoco region.**

Opposite: **Both photographs show the same area of the** *llanos*: **one in the wet season and one in the dry season.**

CLIMATE

Although Venezuela lies completely within the tropical zone, temperatures vary from region to region, depending on elevation and prevailing winds. Lowland areas remain warm throughout the year. The country's highest average annual temperature of 83°F (28°C) occurs in the central part of the *llanos* and the north of the Maracaibo basin. The weather gets much cooler at higher altitudes, and snow covers the highest Andean peaks all year round.

The country basically has three temperature zones. The "hot land" is humid, with average daily temperatures exceeding 75°F (24°C) but rarely topping 95°F (35°C). In the "temperate land," average daily temperatures range from 50 to 80°F (10 to 27°C). In the "cold land," temperatures fall below 65°F (18°C) during the day and reach freezing point at night.

In the wet months, May to October, the *llanos* and forests become swampy and green, but in the dry season, these areas become parched and brown. Rainfall averages less than 20 inches (51 cm) on the mountainous coast. The Orinoco delta and the south of the Maracaibo basin receive up to 80 inches (203 cm) of rain annually. The

plateaus of the Guiana Highlands receive moderate rainfall. Caracas gets about 32 inches (81 cm) a year, as much as Chicago gets.

The national tree of Venezuela, the *aranguery* ("ah-rahn-goo-eh-REE"), grows almost all over the country. When it blooms, it erupts in vibrant yellow flowers that stand out against the green of the rest of the landscape.

FLORA

Venezuela has more plant species than the United States and Canada together have. On mountain slopes below 3,000 feet, tropical forests with dense shrubbery are most common. Scrubby woodland and dense forest filled with exotic orchids—such as the Venezuelan national flower, the deep pink *cattleya mossiae*—cover slopes between 3,000 and 6,000 feet (914.4 and 1,828.8 m). Above 6,000 feet, vegetation is sparse. Grasses and herbaceous plants are most common. In the alpine regions, from 10,000 to 15,000 feet (3,048 to 4,572 m), there is little plant life. The landscape here consists of high pastures freckled with the yellow flowering *frailejón* ("fray-lay-HON") tree. The leaves of this tree resemble rabbits' ears and have been used as mattress stuffing.

In the Maracaibo region, high humidity and heavy rainfall support lush tropical forests. Near the Caribbean Sea, however, the air is drier, and desert plants are more common.

The *llanos* are Venezuela's natural pasture, thanks to light soils and alternating wet and dry seasons. The plains contain more flora than the African grasslands. To the east, in the Orinoco delta, the land is swampy and full of mangrove thickets. Most of the Guiana Highlands is covered with rough natural grass and semideciduous tropical forest tangled with vines and parasitic growth. Unusual plant and animal species and rare orchids populate the 1.8-billion-year-old Mount Roraima, the tallest of the region's *tepuis*, rising 9,219 feet (2,810 m) above sea level.

FAUNA

The Andean Highlands are home to monkeys, bears, deer, wild pigs, otters, sloths, anteaters, foxes, opossums, armadillos, rodents, and big cats such as jaguars, ocelots, and pumas.

The lowlands of the *llanos* compare with the African continent in terms of the variety of wildlife. Many animal species that are threatened elsewhere have survived in the Andean Highlands, because of the absence of a large human population.

Besides the five million cattle that roam the *llanos*, this central region of Venezuela is home to some of the world's most unusual animals. The capybara, which lives in the swampy areas, has the distinction of being the world's largest rodent. It can weigh up to 100 pounds (45.4 kg) and looks more like a friendly beaver or otter than a giant rat. The capybara has partially webbed toes, no tail, and a cleft palate. It eats only plants and communicates by making a low grunting noise.

The Orinoco River contains a great variety of fish, including a species of catfish that can weigh up to 300 pounds (136 kg). Rare river mammals such as the dolphin and sea cow or manatee are also found in the fresh waters of the Orinoco.

The cycnoches chlorochilon *can carry 3.7 million seeds in a single pod. This is to guarantee propagation, since many of the seeds die before they germinate.*

15

The *llanos* are one of the best places in the world to watch birds such as the heron, egret, and brilliant scarlet ibis (*right*), which is found only in northern South America.

The Orinoco dolphin has small eyes, pink skin, a long beak, and a humped back. Unlike other freshwater dolphins, Orinoco dolphins live in schools of 12 to 20 and show signs of group loyalty. A smaller species that grows to only five to six feet (1.5 to 1.8 m) in length is considered sacred by some local Indians. This species has the "smiling" face commonly associated with the ocean-bound bottle-nosed dolphin.

The Orinoco crocodile also makes its home in the *llanos*. The German naturalist Alexander von Humboldt, exploring the Orinoco in the early 1800s, reported seeing crocodiles that measured up to 24 feet (7.3 m) in length. Today, a male Orinoco crocodile may grow up to 16.4 feet (5 m). Between 1920 and 1940, almost two million Orinoco crocodiles were killed for their hides, and they have become one of the most endangered animal species in the world. Despite serious conservation efforts and the collapse of trade in crocodile hides, only 2,000 to 5,000 of these reptiles are left in Venezuela and Colombia.

Every new exploration into the 7.4 million acres (almost 30,000 square km) of jungle in the Guiana Highlands uncovers new animal species never before documented. The harsh terrain and climate have insulated the area from human activity and forced plants and animals indigenous to the region to develop interesting survival traits and tactics. For example, one expedition discovered a species of toad with feet specially adapted for climbing rocky cliffs and a catfish with a full beard used to attract mates.

The giant otter lives in the Orinoco River area.

In the famous Guácharo Cave in northeast Venezuela lives the oilbird, or *guácharo* ("goo-AH-chah-roh"), which has been an object of curiosity since 1799 when Humboldt told the scientific world of its existence. Ten thousand oilbirds live in the Guácharo Cave, within the boundaries of a 34,000-acre (138-square km) reserve.

Oilbirds have reddish-brown feathers. They measure from 12 to 18 inches (30 to 46 cm) in length and have a wing span of more than three feet (0.9 m). Oilbirds are nocturnal, as bats are. During the day, oilbirds sleep crowded together in the black Guácharo Cave. At dusk, they fly out to find food—the oily nut of the palm tree—using echolocation. Most of their waking hours are spent in flight.

The oilbird got its name in the early 1800s when it was hunted by Indians and missionaries for its fat, which was made into lamp oil. Today, it is illegal to kill an oilbird.

17

HISTORY

THE SEARCH FOR GOLD shaped Venezuela's early history, although gold is not the country's main natural resource.

According to myth, a "gilded man," or "El Dorado," made his kingdom in northern South America. This Indian chief was supposed to have been so wealthy that he went about dusted in gold. Every night he washed the gold dust off, and every morning he reapplied it.

With dreams of possessing the kingdom of El Dorado, European explorers traveled to present-day Venezuela in the last years of the 15th century. When Christopher Columbus reached the coast in the 1490s, he wrote to his king and queen to claim the land for Spain and to tell of the Indians he had seen with pearls around their necks and arms.

In 1499, Spanish explorer Alfonso de Ojeda made a memorable expedition to the northern part of Venezuela. Seeing Indian huts built on stilts in Lake Maracaibo, Ojeda and his mapmaker—Amerigo Vespucci, after whom America was named—were reminded of the canals of Venice, so they named the country "Little Venice," or Venezuela.

Above: **Indian huts on stilts in the Orinoco delta.**

Opposite: **A statue of Simon Bolívar, the Liberator, in Caracas.**

THE FIRST INHABITANTS

Like the rest of the Americas, Venezuela was originally inhabited by Indians, who had made their way across the Bering Strait from Asia during the Ice Age. Between 10,000 and 20,000 B.C., South America was populated by hunters who fed on mastodons and giant sloths. By 1000 B.C., these hunters, the peaceful Arawak, had become farmers. They were driven from the land by the warlike Carib.

When Columbus first saw the Indians of Venezuela in October 1492, he described them as being "of tanned color … neither black nor white;" well-built, with "no belly;" and having a broad forehead, straight legs, and black hair that was "straight and coarse like horsehair."

The Venezuelan Indians were accomplished farmers, great artisans, and rich in religious ritual, but they were not as highly organized as the Aztecs, Incas, or Mayas. Although they fought the Spanish *conquistadores* with great spirit, they were overcome.

THE SPANISH CONQUEST

In 1509, the first European settlement in all of South America was founded on the Venezuelan island of Cubagua. The settlers had come in search of pearls, but by 1550 the pearl beds were dry and the island was abandoned. Around 1520, the first permanent Spanish settlement was founded at Cumaná, on the northeastern coast of Venezuela.

The town of Coro, founded in 1527, is significant in Venezuela's history. In order to pay his debts, Charles I of Spain mortgaged the town to the German banking house of Wesler. In search of El Dorado, the Weslers made expeditions into the Venezuelan interior, looting the country and killing many indigenous inhabitants, yet finding no gold. In 1546, Spain terminated its agreement with the Germans and, giving up the search for gold, opted to develop Venezuela agriculturally.

By the end of the 16th century, 20 towns had been established. Many of the Indians were forced to become slaves on the sugar and coffee *haciendas* ("ah-sih-EHN-dahs"), or plantations, of the Spanish settlers. Millions of slaves died, and landowners imported African slaves from the Caribbean islands to work the fields. Although South America had nearly 50 million indigenous Indians in the 15th century, only two million

The Castillo or Fort of San Antonio de la Eminencia was built in 1660 to protect the coastal city of Cumaná from pirates.

survived the conquest. Most of the remaining Indians, who lived in the *llanos* and Maracaibo regions, were colonized by the Dominican, Jesuit, Franciscan, and Augustinian missionaries from Spain who, by the early 1700s, had spread Christianity to remote parts of the country.

The male Spanish settlers, called *peninsulars* ("pay-nihn-SOO-lars"), held powerful positions in the colonies. They eventually married indigenous women, producing *mestizos* ("mehs-TEE-sohs"), children of Spanish and Indian parentage. *Criollos* ("kree-OH-lohs"), or Creoles, were people of Spanish heritage born in Venezuela. They held prominent positions at the local level and resented the dominant class of *peninsulars*. The *criollos* also intermarried. People of African origin who were brought over as slaves were considered the lowest class.

Evidence of the Spanish conquest is found in Venezuela's forts and religious institutions. La Casa Fuerte in Barcelona was originally the Convent of San Francisco.

THE INDEPENDENCE MOVEMENT

Like the U.S. independence movement, the Venezuelan movement had its roots in the desire of Venezuelans to trade freely with other nations.

In 1728, the Real Compañia Guipuzcoana de Caracas was established, giving the Basques from Spain exclusive rights to import goods into Venezuela. In 1785, however, because of local jealousy and opposition to the monopoly of foreign trade by the Europeans, the company was dismantled and free trade was granted, but only within the Spanish Empire.

In 1797, Britain occupied the island of Trinidad for the purpose of selling goods illegally to Venezuela. To foil British attempts, Spain decided to allow free trade among all nations. However, in 1802, the Spaniards changed their minds and decided once again to limit free trade. Led by *caraqueño* Francisco de Miranda, many angry Venezuelans revolted, beginning the independence movement.

This initial foray into self-rule was not successful, however, and Miranda was exiled. He returned in 1810 and, the following year, was proclaimed dictator of Venezuela. The country then had a population of about 700,000, 60 percent of African heritage. Miranda's dictatorship was short-lived, however. By 1812, he was captured by forces still in favor of Spanish rule.

Simón Bolívar, also a *caraqueño* and Miranda's former aide, invaded Venezuela in 1813, reestablished the republic, appointing himself as dictator, and gained the title of Liberator. Unfortunately, the republic was destroyed again in 1814 by a group of plains cowboys, or *llaneros*, who still had royalist leanings. Bolívar was forced into exile but returned in 1817 to establish the third republic.

In 1819, Bolívar devised a grand scheme to bring what are now Venezuela, Ecuador, and Colombia together to form one independent state; Gran Colombia. It was not until 1821, however, that Bolívar accomplished his scheme by defeating the Spanish at Carabobo.

In 1830, Venezuela seceded from Gran Colombia and became truly independent. José Antonio Páez, who had expelled the last Spanish garrison in 1823, was named president.

Simón Bolívar's plans for "Gran Colombia" included Venezuela, Colombia, and Ecuador.

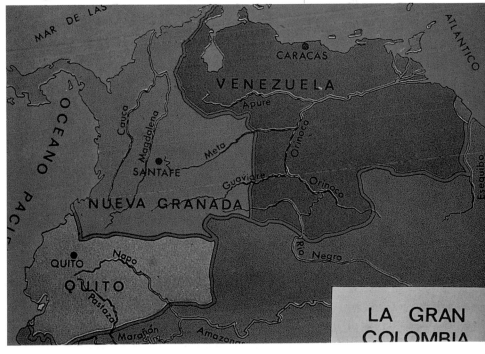

SIMÓN BOLÍVAR, THE LIBERATOR

Simón Bolívar is Venezuela's most revered citizen. Born in Caracas to wealthy *criollo* parents in 1783, Bolívar traveled to Europe in 1799 and 1803. In France, he was influenced by the revolutionary spirit of the Parisians, who inspired his dream of independence for Venezuela.

Bolívar was a thin, small man, with a lean face and vibrant black eyes. A good horseman and swimmer, he had an amazing amount of energy. His soldiers were devoted to him, and the British Romantic poet, Lord Byron, was so enamored of him that he named his boat *Bolivar* and actually made plans to move to Venezuela with his daughter.

Bolívar was a brilliant orator, and his speeches are still read and respected today. In 1812, when Caracas was destroyed by an earthquake, he said, "If Nature opposes our designs, we shall fight against her and make her obey." Bolívar died in 1830 at age 47.

THE TURBULENT ROAD TO DEMOCRACY

From 1908 to 1935, Venezuela was dominated by a fierce dictator. With the army and police under his control, General Juan Vicente Gómez ruled by repression and terror. The years between 1936 and 1948 enjoyed democratic rule and the election to the presidency of the country's most famous novelist, Rómulo Gallegos. Political unrest followed, and from 1950 to 1958, Venezuela fell under the control of another dictator, General Marcos Pérez Jiménez. His tenure was marked by corruption and brutal suppression of the opposition, though he did make contributions, building roads and housing projects in Caracas.

It was not until 1958 that Rómulo Betancourt and his democratic party, Acción Democrática (AD), brought lasting democracy to Venezuela.

Betancourt is famous for his philosophy of "sowing the oil," or using petroleum profits for the benefit of the people. Betancourt tackled social problems such as illiteracy, poor living conditions and education facilities, and a high infant mortality rate.

Carlos Andrés Pérez was elected president in 1974 and again in 1989. He nationalized the petroleum industry and launched ambitious programs in education and agriculture. In foreign relations, Venezuela, through Pérez, has become an important advocate of human rights and economic independence. Pérez survived two military coup attempts before being tried in 1993 on charges of misappropriating $17 million in government funds; he was suspended permanently from the presidency.

In 1993, Rafael Caldera led his Convergencia coalition party to election victory, breaking the decades-long hold on power of AD and the Social Christian Party (COPEI). In 1994, President Caldera responded to a financial crisis involving the collapse of several banks by suspending civil liberties, which were restored in 1995, except in turbulent border zones. The 1995 municipal and regional elections saw a voter turnout of only 40 percent and the decline of Caldera's popularity.

In the 1998 elections, Hugo Chávez Frías of the Fifth Republic Movement (MVR) rode to power on a wave of popular support. He appealed to the working classes by promising improved workers' rights, constitutional changes, and an anti-corruption drive. In 1999, a National Constituent Assembly (ANC) replaced the senate and congress. Chávez supporters won 90 percent of the 131 seats. The ANC proposed a new constitution, approved by more than 70 percent of voters.

In the 2000 elections, Chávez beat former ally Francisco Arias Cardenas, but his Patriotic Pole alliance won 60 percent of the National Constituent Assembly seats, not quite enough to form a majority.

"I will never allow my hands to be idle or my soul to rest until I have broken the shackles which chain us to Spain."

—Simón Bolívar, as a student in Europe

GOVERNMENT

THE REPUBLIC OF VENEZUELA is one of Latin America's oldest functioning democracies. It is made up of 23 states, the Federal District of Caracas, and a Federal Dependency consisting of 72 islands organized into 11 federally controlled groups. In 1985, the states were subdivided into 156 districts and 613 municipalities.

NATIONAL GOVERNMENT

Like the U.S. government, the Venezuelan government can be divided into three branches: the executive, legislative, and judicial.

The executive branch consists of a cabinet of ministers headed by the president, who is both chief of state and head of government. The president is elected for a six-year term and may be reelected for a second consecutive term. He or she works in conjunction with the congress—the legislative branch—to determine the size and composition of the cabinet. The president also appoints the vice-president, subject to approval by the congress.

Other presidential duties include: making and ratifying international treaties, conventions, and agreements; directing foreign affairs; commanding the armed forces; calling a state of emergency when necessary; ordering the suspension of constitutional guarantees when necessary; and introducing and defending bills before the congress.

Under the 1999 constitution, the former bicameral congress consisting of a senate and chamber of deputies was replaced by a single-chamber congress, the National Assembly.

Opposite: **The Capitol, the government building in Caracas.**

Below: **The Elliptic Salon of the Federal Palace in Caracas, on the ceiling of which is painted the Battle of Carabobo, the scene of Simón Bolívar's victory.**

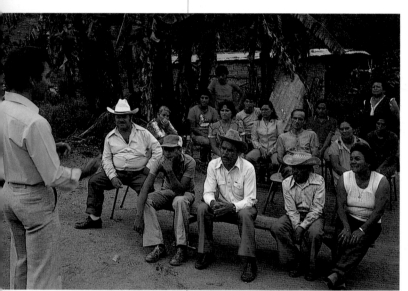

A government spokes-person gives a talk on "intelligence develop-ment" as part of government plans to educate Venezuelans in remote regions IIke Trujillo.

Members of the National Assembly are elected by popular vote to serve five-year terms; a few seats are reserved for representatives of indigenous Venezuelans.

The National Assembly has the power to approve, amend, or reject legislation proposed by the executive branch. The president can, however, veto bills passed by the National Assembly or order the congress to reconsider amendments made to proposed legislation.

The president can also dissolve the National Assembly in times of crisis or if the National Assembly twice rejects the presidential choice for vice-president. However, the National Assembly can, with a two-thirds majority, override the president's veto.

The judicial branch of the Venezuelan government consists of the Supreme Court of Justice. The National Assembly elects the 18 members of the supreme court for 12-year terms. Supreme court justices serve only one term.

The Supreme Court of Justice holds ultimate judicial power; it is the highest court in the land, and its decisions cannot be appealed. It can declare a law or an act of the president unconstitutional, and it can determine whether the president and members of the National Assembly can be put on trial.

Each state has its own supreme court as well as lower courts. The judicial council selects judges for the lower civilian courts.

A council consisting of the public prosecutor, general accountant, and defender of the people (a national ombudsman) investigates acts against the public's interest and works to ensure the legal use of public funds.

VOTING

Voting in presidential elections is compulsory for all Venezuelans over the age of 18. Soldiers are also entitled to vote. Elections are organized and

Venezuelan soldiers on parade in Caracas.

supervised by the National Electoral Council (CNE), which consists of five members elected by the National Assembly for a seven-year term.

The constitution guarantees the freedom to form political parties. A party must obtain one percent of the national vote in order to retain its legal status. The major parties include Democratic Action (AD), Fifth Republic Movement (MVR), the Social Christian party (COPEI), Homeland for All (PPT), Movement to Socialism (MAS), and Convergencia.

LOCAL GOVERNMENT

Individual states in Venezuela elect their own legislatures, but have limited powers. They operate on funds allocated by the national government and abide by laws and decisions made by the National Assembly on education, health, and agricultural issues. The states are divided into districts and municipalities run by city councils. State governors and council members are elected by their constituents.

THE VENEZUELAN CONSTITUTION

The first Venezuelan constitution was adopted on December 21, 1811, almost six months after independence from Spain. The original document was influenced by, but not based on the U.S. and French constitutions.

Since 1811, the constitution has been rewritten 25 times, usually in response to political upheaval. The 22nd constitution, adopted in 1945, gave women the right to vote, and the 23rd version, adopted in 1947, separated Church from State and increased the authority of the federal government. The 24th constitution, adopted in 1953, changed the country's official name to the Republic of Venezuela. The 25th constitution, adopted in 1999, renamed the country the Bolivarian Republic of Venezuela.

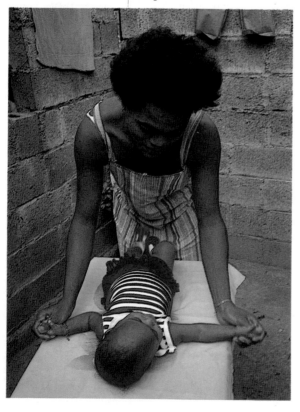

In Maracaibo, a mother helps her baby exercise, as taught by a government social worker.

Like the U.S. constitution, the Venezuelan constitution advocates personal liberties and human equality. The introduction states that all Venezuelans have the right to social and legal equality, "without discrimination due to race, sex, creed, or social conditions." One of the constitution's aims is to support democracy as the sole means of ensuring the rights and dignity of citizens. The constitution also refers to Simón Bolívar as the Liberator of Venezuela.

Two articles of the constitution proclaim the right to freedom of religion and expression, and another allows for freedom of peaceful assembly. The constitution requires that the State provide an education for all citizens as well as oversee the maintenance of public health. The government promises to try to improve the living conditions of the rural population and to protect the Indian communities and help them integrate into the life of the nation.

In return, the constitution declares that the State expects all Venezuelans to "honor and defend their country and to safeguard and protect the interests of the Nation." Military service is compulsory, as is education, and "labor is a duty of every person fit to perform it."

The 1999 constitution ratified the replacement of the senate by a unicameral National Assembly, created the post of vice-president, and combined the military forces under one commander.

Hugo Chávez Frías, president of Venezuela.

THE GOVERNMENT'S GOALS

The goals of the Venezuelan government include: preserving free and democratic institutions and maintaining public order; strengthening and modernizing the armed forces; upgrading law enforcement; eliminating social conditions that foster crime; refinancing debt owed to other nations without excessively affecting the living standards of Venezuelans.

The government is actively seeking to control inflation and revitalize the economy by improving the physical infrastructure to encourage agricultural development, by attracting new foreign investment through joint ventures with local companies and access to previously restricted areas, and by reducing intervention in business and industry.

ECONOMY

IN THE LATE 1970s, during President Carlos Andrés Pérez's first term, Venezuela was at the height of economic prosperity. Oil revenues were pouring in; new petrochemical, steel, and hydroelectric plants were being built; ships from other countries were lining up at Venezuelan ports to unload luxury items imported for *caraqueños*; and the wealthiest Venezuelans were traveling abroad on shopping sprees or leaving to study at foreign universities.

By the early 1980s, the economic scene had completely changed. A worldwide oil glut had reduced Venezuela's oil revenues, crippling the nation's ability to settle its foreign debt; local prices rose dramatically, while salaries were frozen or jobs lost; even food staples like salt, rice, and sugar became difficult to obtain.

The Venezuelan economy has been dominated by petroleum since the discovery of oil in 1914. Oil revenues formerly made up more than two-thirds of the government's income and more than 90 percent of the country's exports. Such a heavy reliance on petroleum exports meant that when oil revenues fell, the entire economy collapsed. Although the Venezuelan economy has recovered to some extent, the country has had to refocus, to try to develop industries that depend less on petroleum.

The government has four goals for advancing economic recovery: (1) to reduce the number of government workers by transferring the provision of public services to private companies; (2) to remove laws that obstruct efficiency and competition; (3) to encourage foreign companies to invest in Venezuela; and (4) to shift the economy away from oil and into new export industries like steel, gold, cocoa, coffee, fruit, and petrochemicals. The government also aims to encourage tourism, especially to the fine beaches of Margarita Island and the modern shopping malls and classy restaurants of Caracas.

Opposite: **A fruitseller cycles his fresh produce around a market area in Venezuela.**

33

The Ciudad Guayana Industrial Complex produces iron ore, paper, and aluminum.

FACTS AND FIGURES

Earnings from petrochemicals, oil refining, manufacturing, construction, and trade make up 63 percent of Venezuela's gross domestic product (GDP). Agricultural products, which make up four percent of the GDP, include corn, sorghum, sugarcane, rice, bananas, vegetables, coffee, beef, pork, milk, eggs, and fish. Exports include petroleum, bauxite, aluminum, steel, chemicals, and agricultural and manufactured products. Imports include machinery and equipment, transportation equipment, raw materials, and construction materials. In 1999, Venezuela exported $20.9 billion worth of goods and imported $11.8 billion worth of goods. The country trades with the United States, Puerto Rico, Colombia, Brazil, Japan, France, Germany, the Netherlands, Italy, and Canada.

PETROLEUM AND MINING

Before the discovery of petroleum in Lake Maracaibo, Venezuela was a relatively poor country of farmers, and many consumer goods had to be imported. Once oil was discovered, however, rapid changes took place, bringing immense wealth to the country, though not to most of the people. Foreign companies were invited to exploit Venezuelan oil reserves and to process extracted oil, and the dictators in power in Venezuela at the time hoarded the wealth and made handsome profits for themselves.

When Rómulo Betancourt took control of the government in 1959, he used the accumulated profits from the oil industry to fund desperately needed social programs. He directed foreign oil companies to train Venezuelans and to pay a higher percentage of their profits to the Venezuelan government. Before the 1960s, most of Venezuela's oil was refined outside the country. Venezuela now has its own refineries, and gas is saved for fuel and other uses.

About 75 percent of the nation's oil comes from the Lake Maracaibo region. Other reserves are in the northern *llanos*, in the Apure-Barinas river basin in the west, and in the eastern region. These deposits will not last forever, of course, and the country is exploring the Orinoco delta and offshore locations for new oil deposits.

The most important natural resource in Venezuela after petroleum is iron ore, much of which is used in the local steel industry, as are nickel, zinc, and coal. Bauxite, discovered in the 1970s, is used in the aluminum industry.

"Our country is rich but our people are poor."

—ex-President Carlos Andrés Pérez

A sponge-iron mill in Orinoco. Sponge iron is derived from iron ore through a reduction process.

The Guri Dam at the Caroní River.

MANUFACTURING AND POWER GENERATION

Venezuela's early attempts at industrial diversification included the manufacture of aluminum products in Ciudad Guayana. Factories in Caracas manufacture glass, chemicals, leather goods, pharmaceuticals, and processed food. Venezuela also manufactures steel, textiles, clothing, tobacco, paper, and cars, among other products. In 2000, manufacturing contributed 20 percent of the country's GDP, and manufacturing output increased by 3.6 percent.

Venezuela has huge electric power dams on the Caroní River, and Venezuelans enjoy one of the best electrical energy services in Latin America. Power outages or electrical surges occur much less frequently in Venezuela than in neighboring countries.

AGRICULTURE

Venezuela neglected its agricultural potential during the oil boom in the 1970s. Eggs came from Florida, meat from Argentina, and vegetables from Chile. While in the 1930s, the agricultural sector contributed 70 percent of the GDP, it accounted for only 4 percent of the GDP in the late 1990s, when it exported $630.2 million and imported $1.782 billion worth of food.

With the fall in oil prices and the ensuing economic crisis, came plans to exploit Venezuela's agricultural potential. Unfortunately, by 1988, only about 13 percent of the population was still engaged in agriculture. Many had already moved to urban areas in pursuit of jobs away from the soil.

The government is now encouraging people to become farmers by providing them with credit, technical assistance, and machinery, but many young people prefer to stay in the cities. Some progress has been made in cattle-breeding on the *llanos* and in the cultivation of cocoa, coffee, and tropical fruit elsewhere. With less than 5 percent of the country's arable land being cultivated and many unemployed urban dwellers, Venezuela still has a long way to go to reaching full agricultural development.

Above: **A fisherman dries a fresh catch on the shore.**

Left: **A herder in the Maracaibo basin drives cattle to the market.**

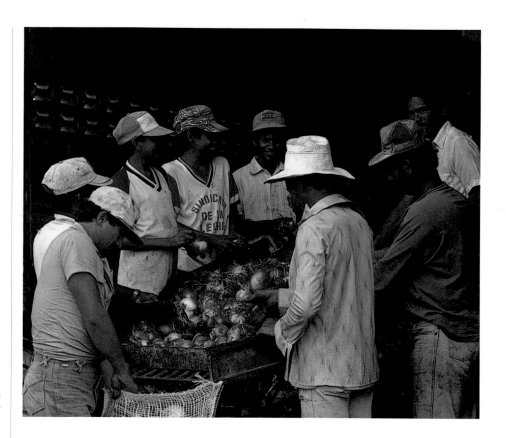

Workers sort out the onion crop in the Lake Valencia basin.

THE VENEZUELAN WORK FORCE

The Venezuelan work force is made up of about 10.5 million people, with an unemployment rate of around 15 percent. About 61.4 percent of the work force is in services; 26.9 percent in manufacturing; and 11.8 percent in agriculture. About 18 percent of the work force belongs to unions, which are particularly strong in the petroleum and public sectors.

The minimum monthly wage is $200. Slightly more than 80 percent of households earn over $5,000 a year. Purchasing power is quite low, as most households tend to be very large.

The class structure in Venezuela is quite rigid. The upper class works mostly in business. Before the 20th century, this elite group made their money in agriculture. They owned large cocoa, sugar, or coffee plantations, using African and *mestizo* laborers. Many members of the upper class now own family businesses.

The middle class has grown considerably since the discovery of petroleum and the subsequent creation of new jobs. Members of the middle class, most of whom are city dwellers, typically work in technology, business management, education, the priesthood, and the government. Most advertising is aimed at middle-class Venezuelans, as they are most likely to buy consumer goods and housing.

The lower class is mostly rural and makes up the majority of the population. Members of this class are often employed as subsistence farmers, farm workers, sharecroppers, domestic servants, or in other manual occupations.

In Caracas, members of the lower class often work in factories. To earn more money, many work the night shift over and above the minimum 40-hour week. Others work in the construction industry, which is based in Caracas. Many laborers belong to the Confederation of Venezuelan Workers, a trade union with more than 1.5 million members.

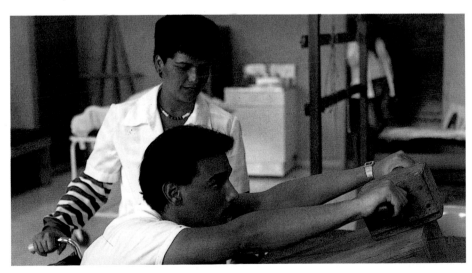

An occupational therapist helps a patient recuperate at a hospital in Caracas.

DOING BUSINESS IN VENEZUELA

Venezuelan businesspeople are typically quite sophisticated, well-educated, and accustomed to dealing with people from other cultures. They work in modern, air-conditioned offices, using up-to-date technology, and they wear well-cut suits to work everyday.

Venezuelan businesspeople are generally more aware of organizational hierarchies than their counterparts from the United States are. In the office, Venezuelans show respect for their superiors by, for example, holding the door open for them and never interrupting or arguing with them. Senior executives have the privilege of speaking first in a meeting and making the final decision.

Business discussions are often formal. Venezuelans do not take kindly to impatient foreigners who fidget in their seat, dominate the conversation, or try to force everyone into a quick decision. The typical Venezuelan businessperson takes time to assess issues before voicing an idea, so that he or she can back down or change position without attracting too much attention. Many Americans have a different way of doing business. They pay little attention to rank, "get down to business" as soon as everyone is seated at the conference table, and sell their products or ideas with a lot of vigor and enthusiasm.

Venezuelans work hard, but they also believe in making time for the traditional Latin American siesta, or midday rest. The normal business day in Venezuela begins at 8 A.M. and ends at 6 P.M., Monday through Friday. There is a two-hour lunch break at noon, and many people go home for a large meal and a quick nap. Stores are usually open from 9 A.M. to 1 P.M. and then from 3 P.M. to 7 P.M. Banks remain open to public from 8:30 A.M. to 3:30 P.M. Restaurants also usually stay open through the siesta hours. Many Venezuelans leave work early on Friday afternoons.

Opposite: **A view of Caracas. The capital of Venezuela, the financial and business center of the country, is growing faster than any other Latin American capital.**

41

ENVIRONMENT

VENEZUELA HAS SOME 208,440 SQUARE MILES (540,000 square km) of forested and wooded land, 70 percent of which consists of the Amazon Basin in the south of the country. Each year, human activity clears almost 2,316 square miles (6,000 square km) of the country's forests—mangrove and inland swamps, montane and lowland rain forests, dry forests, and other forests. This represents an annual loss of 1.31 percent of the country's total forest cover—one of the highest rates of deforestation in the tropics.

While there are zones of protected forest scattered throughout Venezuela, the total area protected is only just over 44,776 square miles (116,000 square km). The country's 43 national parks, managed by the National Park Institute (INPARQUES), showcase an impressive variety of natural habitats and species of wildlife. INPARQUES has information offices in all the national parks and restricts access or charges entry fees to some. While national park status may not guarantee protection, many parks are valued also as tourist destinations. There are thus both environmental and economic motives for the preservation of such parks.

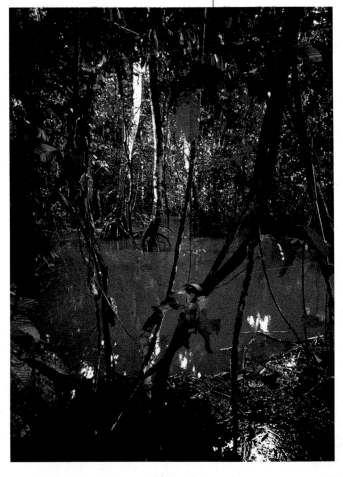

Below: **A swamp area in the Amazon.**

Opposite: **Hacha Falls viewed from the lagoon in the Canalma National Park.**

SOME OF VENEZUELA'S PARKS

HENRI PITTIER NATIONAL PARK in the state of Aragua is Venezuela's oldest national park, founded in 1937. It has an area of 416 square miles (1,078 square km).

CUEVA DEL GUÁCHARO in Monagas and Sucre has the famous cave of oilbirds and premontane and humid forests filled with many animals, notably pumas and yellow-knobbed curassows.

TURUÉPANO in Sucre was created to protect the manatee. The last of Venezuela's "mermaids" live in the Gulf of Paria between the island of Turuépano and the mainland.

MOCHIMA in Anzoátegui and Sucre is over 363 square miles (940 square km) of mountainous coast and islands. The Pampero Ecological Foundation aims to protect the park through measuring its resources and levels of use, making recommendations for sustainable levels of exploitation. Many species of tropical fish thrive in the park's waters.

MÉDANOS DE CORO in Falcón is a compact desert, complete with wind-sculpted dunes.

MORROCOY also in Falcón is over 124 square miles (320 square km) of coral reefs and mangrove swamps. Its beauty and resident flamingos make it very popular with tourists.

ARCHIPIÉLAGO DE LOS ROQUES in Dependencias Federales consists of islands, islets, keys, lagoons, and beaches with rich marine fauna. The Scientific Foundation of Los Roques protects the endangered green turtle on the island of Dos Mosquises Sur.

LAGUNA DE LA RESTINGA, 41 square miles (107 square km) dominated by mangrove swamps, boasts flamingos, pelicans, and scarlet ibis.

SIERRA NEVADA in Mérida and Barinas covers rain forests, high plains, and snowcapped peaks, such as Pico Bolívar. There is a breeding center for the Andean condor here.

SIERRA LA CULATA has a valley running north of Mérida into the Andes. In this rocky terrain live jaguars, tapirs, and spectacled bears.

PARIMA-TAPIRAPECÓ is the fifth largest national park in the world at nearly 15,440 square miles (40,000 square m). Most of the Yanomami of Venezuela live here. The Sierra Parima mountains and the headwaters of the Orinoco are features of the park.

SERRANÍA DE LA NEBLINA contains the world's largest *tepui*, through which runs the Cañon Grande de Río Baría, one of the deepest canyons in the world.

EL ÁVILA in Distrito Federal, Miranda, and Vargas overlooks Caracas and is a popular hiking destination. Many animals, including armadillos and sloths, live here.

YURUBÍ in Yaracuy has cloud forests in the Sierra de Aroa, which conceal orchids, boa constrictors, and red brocket deer, among many other species.

SIERRA DE PERIJÁ in Zulia consists of cloud forests and high plains. This park is inhabited by the capuchin monkey and king vulture.

CIÉNAGAS DEL CATATUMBO in Zulia is home to the jabiru stork, blue heron, great egret, and many other birds that live on the delta of the Catatumbo River along Lake Maracaibo.

MARIUSA in Delta Amacuro is located in the middle of the Orinoco delta. The Warau people inhabit this park's dense jungle.

NATURAL RESOURCES

Venezuela is blessed with such natural resources as diamonds, iron ore, and especially petroleum, natural gas, and coal. The country is also one of the world's top bauxite and aluminum producers.

It has been estimated that Venezuelan reserves hold 77 billion barrels of oil, 1.2 trillion barrels of bitumen in the Orinoco belt, and 146.8 trillion cubic feet of natural gas. The country's refineries have the capacity to produce more than a million barrels of oil a day, and Venezuela aims to raise its crude oil output to 5.5 million tons (5,500 million kg) by 2006. Venezuela is the third largest producer of coal in South America, after Colombia and Brazil. Most of its coal reserves are found near the border with Colombia.

Hydropower is another major natural resource in Venezuela, generating about 70 percent of the country's electricity supply, which was 81.2 billion kilowatthours in 1999. The rest of the domestic electricity supply is derived from oil and natural gas.

The beauty of Venezuela's natural environment is an important resource that has drawn tourists to the country.

Interesting bird species populate Venezuela's coastlines.

ENVIRONMENTAL LAW

Venezuela's environment ministry is responsible for, among other tasks, managing national parks and conserving wildlife in the country and monitoring and regulating the exploitation of the country's natural resources.

The ministry can punish those whose activities degrade the environment. It seizes equipment belonging to offenders and imposes penalties ranging from imprisonment to fines to community service. The ministry can also authorize activities that yield definite economic and social benefits, provided they do not harm the environment irreparably. In such cases, guarantees and procedures for the repair of environmental damage must be established in advance.

The Environment Act enacted in 1976 promotes public and private participation in domestic environmental protection and government participation in international agreements on biodiversity, climate change, endangered species, hazardous waste, marine life conservation, the nuclear test ban, and ozone layer protection.

PROBLEMS

Venezuela's environmental problems include pollution and deforestation. Pollution from consumption and energy production is high, because production is the engine of the economy and consumption is heavily subsidized by the government. Carbon emissions are higher in Venezuela than in its South American neighbors, largely due to its active hydrocarbon industries and heavy energy subsidization. Oil exploration, sewage dumping, and fertilizer run-off cause severe pollution in the country's rivers and lakes.

A caiman in the Amazon.

The use of renewable energy resources, apart from hydropower, is low in Venezuela. The few domestic renewable energy projects that have been successful have used solar energy to supply electricity to remote areas where companies are exploring for new oil reserves.

A study done by the Simón Bolívar University found that a new development—an international airport and 150 hotels—would have detrimental effects on the Morrocoy National Park on the eastern coast of Falcón State. In particular danger is Tacarigua Lagoon, home to 140 American crocodiles, an endangered species. However, the tourism corporation, CORPOTURISMO, commissioned a second study that gave the green light to proceed with the development plan.

Amazonas State is home to 40,000 indigenous people from the Guajibo, Makiritare, Piaroa, Guaiaca, and Yanomami groups. National parks in this state occupy 23,160 square miles (60,000 square km), and only one of these parks is open to the public. Of the 8,000 plant species found in Amazonas, 7,000 are endemic.

THREATS TO INDIGENOUS LANDS

In 1993, representatives of the 19 Amazonian groups of Venezuela held the first Congress of Indigenous Peoples of the Amazon. This resulted in the formation of the Organizacion Regional de Pueblos Indigenas de Amazonas (ORPIA), a democratic organization committed to defending and promoting the interests of indigenous peoples.

Although a government decree in Venezuela guarantees the rights of indigenous peoples to their ancestral lands, 72 percent of indigenous Indians still do not have any legal title to their lands. In any case, indigenous land rights often tend to be ignored when logging and mining licences are issued.

One significant development that threatens the welfare of indigenous Indians in Venezuela is the government's decision to exploit mineral and biological resources in the Imataca Forest Reserve. The 13,896-square-mile (36,000-square-km) reserve is home to over 10,000 Akawaio, Arawako, Karina, and Pemon Indians as well as many species of wildlife, some endemic. In 1997, the government signed Decree 1850, which opened up 40 percent of the reserve to industrial mining and logging operations. The indigenous inhabitants, claiming ancestral rights to the land and objecting to pollution and land degradation caused by mining and forestry, have clashed with small- and medium-scale miners and developers who have already entered the area and with multinationals to come.

The government has also planned an electrical line through the Guayana region, 55 percent of which will pass through the Canaima National Park as well as the Imataca Forest Reserve. Building the line will involve the erection of 400 towers along a 459-foot (140-m) corridor. The line will pass through several indigenous communities, despite their opposition. In 1998, Pemon Indians set up roadblocks in protest, but their bows and arrows were no match for rubber bullets and tear gas the national guard used to break up the demonstration. In the next two years, the Pemon Indians knocked down twelve pylons.

In Amazonas State, mining has hurt Yanomami Indians in the Upper Orinoco–Casiquiare Biosphere Reserve, the largest area of protected rain forest in the world. The area is already being illegally exploited by both Venezuelan and Brazilian gold miners. Much of Venezuela's gold is near the surface, making it easy and economical to extract. To get at the gold, miners conveniently clear the topsoil and vegetation by spraying jets of water from powerful pumps that draw the water from nearby rivers.

Mining has caused deforestation and mercury poisoning in the lands of Kapon and Pemon Indians in Bolívar State. In 1996, several species of fish had to be banned from human consumption due to high levels of mercury detected in the Guri Dam.

Deforestation strips the land of natural vegetation to make way for industry.

VENEZUELANS

VENEZUELANS ARE UNITED in language, religion, and loyalty to country; From blue-eyed, blond-haired descendants of German immigrants to dark-eyed, dark-haired descendants of indigenous Indians, all are *Venezolanos* ("beh-neh-zoh-LAH-nohs"). From Latin last names such as Martinez and Pérez to European last names such as Jordan and Vollmar, all belong to *Venezolanos*.

Venezuelans have intermarried since colonial times. A 69-percent majority are *mestizos*, people of mixed ethnicity. *Mestizos* live throughout the country, in both urban and rural areas. People of European descent, mostly Spanish and German, make up 20 percent of the population. They live mainly in the cities. People of African origin make up 9 percent of the population, and indigenous Indians make up the remaining 2 percent of the population. Most African Venezuelans live in the northern coastal regions, while Indians live in the south or on the Colombian border.

About 2 percent of the Venezuelan population are legal immigrants. It is estimated that there are more than two million illegal immigrants in the country. Most are Colombians who work in the construction industry in Caracas or in the petroleum industry in Maracaibo.

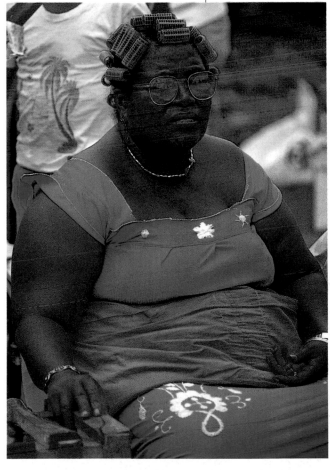

Opposite and below: **Mestizo** *and* **African Venezuelans.**

POPULATION DISTRIBUTION

In 2000, there were 23.5 million people living in Venezuela. The country experienced a population boom in the 1920s, after the discovery of petroleum in Maracaibo, and again in the 1950s. After World War II, the availability of jobs in Venezuela attracted more than 500,000 immigrants from Italy, Spain, Portugal, France, Poland, and Germany.

Oil revenues have given the Venezuelan people better health care services. This has helped lower the country's death rate while maintaining a high birth rate. Whereas in the 1930s, 18 in 1,000 Venezuelans died each year, by 2000 the annual death rate had dropped to five in 1,000.

Venezuela's birth rate at the start of the 21st century was 21 in 1,000, compared to 17.2 in 1,000 for Chile and about 19 in 1,000 for Argentina and Brazil. Life expectancy is about 73 years; most Venezuelans die of "modern" diseases such as heart disease, rather than contagious diseases that still cause many deaths in less developed countries.

The Venezuelan population grew annually by 3.6 percent in the 1960s; by 2000 the growth rate had fallen to 2.1 percent. Despite family planning encouraged by the government, the population growth rate remains high.

Between 1995 and 2000, Venezuela's urban population grew by more than two percent, while the rural population declined. The cities and towns, each with more than 1,000 people, support 87 percent of the national population. Only 13 percent of Venezuelans live in the rural areas.

Citizens of Mérida. Nearly 90 percent of Venezuelans live in cities and towns.

CLASS STRUCTURE

For centuries, a deep-rooted class structure divided Venezuelan society into just two classes of people: the wealthy Europeans and the rest. Before the discovery of oil in the 1920s, about 70 percent of Venezuelans were illiterate rural peasants. By the 1980s, demographic trends had reversed, with more than 80 percent of the population in the literate urban category. The move away from traditional society speeded up in the 1940s, with a burgeoning middle class.

Class distinctions persist in modern Venezuela, and there is a wide gap between rich and poor. Wealth, family background, and cultural accomplishments set the minority upper class apart. Their ethnic heritage is European, and many of them are well-educated and well-traveled. The women are very elegant; few of them pursue careers, and most have household servants.

The middle class is made up of educated people of mixed ethnic backgrounds. Much of their social life revolves around their occupations. Manual laborers and farmers make up the lower class. They often live in small villages, forming tight communities. Social life revolves around planting, harvesting, and religious ceremonies.

"The poor man knows how poor he is. He has his transistor radio."

—*ex-President Pérez*

Above: **Orinoco Indians in a makeshift home.**

A church in Colonia Tovar, a town in a fertile valley.

GERMANY IN VENEZUELA

In the 1830s, after wars stripped the countryside of farmers and slaves, the Venezuelan government encouraged people from Europe to migrate to Venezuela. Two mapmakers, Agustín Codazzi from Italy and Alexander Benitz from Germany, came up with an idea to send a group of German peasants to an area near Caracas, where they could settle down and hopefully prosper. The desired land belonged to a wealthy aristocrat named Manuel Felipe de Tovar. Tovar donated the piece of land to the establishment of the new colony, Colonia Tovar.

A school, church, and pharmacy were built, and a printing press brought in to publish news in Spanish and German. Benitz recruited people from the Schwarzwald, or Black Forest, in Germany. Envisioning a completely self-sufficient colony, Benitz selected artisans, doctors, teachers, and farmers to form the migrant community. A group of 374 men, women, and children set out for Venezuela in 1843. Unfortunately, 70 of them died of smallpox on board the ship.

The remaining immigrants landed on an open beach. There were no roads leading up the mountains to their destination, so they had to climb

A resident of the immigrant settlement of Colonia Tovar.

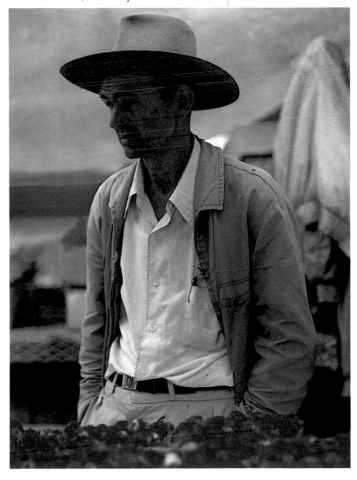

on foot. More died along the way, but the survivors found a glorious place with a perfect climate waiting for them. They soon settled down and waited for more of their countrymen to join them. Unfortunately, none came, and the new colonists were forgotten by the Venezuelan government. They remained isolated for over 80 years and retained the German language and customs they had brought with them. Only in 1963 was a proper road built from Caracas, making Colonia Tovar more accessible.

Colonia Tovar is now a popular tourist destination as well as an agricultural center. Venezuelans and foreigners visit the town to see Bavarian-style architecture, watch authentic German dance, and eat German sausage, sauerkraut, Black Forest cake, and locally cultivated strawberries, apples, and peaches.

THE INDIANS OF VENEZUELA

From around 500,000 at the time of the Spanish conquest, the indigenous population has dwindled to 316,000, making up just one percent of the national population. Many of Venezuela's indigenous Indians live in the most inaccessible areas, such as the Orinoco delta, the rain forests that spread south into Brazil and west into Colombia, and the desert-like Guajira Peninsula just north of Maracaibo.

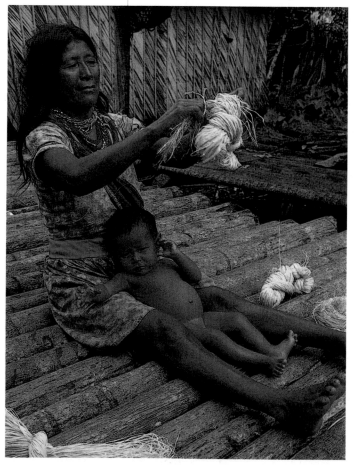

A Warau Indian prepares palm fibers to weave a hammock.

Guajiro Indians make up the largest indigenous group in Venezuela. They speak their own language, wear distinctive, colorful clothes, and follow ancient customs and rituals. Some, however, have left their desert homes to pursue jobs in Maracaibo. These have assimilated into urban society, working in the oil and construction industries or selling fruit and vegetables at outdoor markets.

Those who stay in their homeland lead a semi-nomadic lifestyle; they live in temporary homes, which they leave when food and water run out. Many Guajiros have intermarried, but they retain their culture and identity, and many children of mixed marriages think of themselves as Guajiro rather than *mestizo*. Guajiros educated in the

Indians of the state of Zulia (*left*) and the Orinoco delta (*below*).

city often return to the peninsula to resume their former way of life.

At least 12 different Indian groups live in the Amazonas Federal Territory near the Brazilian border. Each has its own language and culture.

The Makiritare or Yekuana people live on rivers and use 54-foot-long (16.5-m-long) dugout canoes made from tree trunks as transportation vehicles. The Piaroa build 36-foot-high (11-m-high) conical houses thatched with palm fronds. The warlike Yanomami are one of the most isolated groups in Venezuela and Brazil; many of them have never seen a human being with fair skin. Warau Indians live in the Orinoco River delta; they are skilled fishermen and navigators and build their homes on stilts.

DRESS HABITS

In Caracas and other large cities, upper- and upper-middle-class people dress conservatively. The men wear suits, white shirts, and ties; the women wear dresses, skirts and blouses, or suits. Businesswomen wear makeup and dress elegantly, with jewelry and high heels, but they never wear revealing clothing.

At night, people dress formally for dining out or going to the theater. Men wear jackets and ties; women wear cocktail dresses, often with designer labels. Jeans and casual clothing are worn on the streets. Shorts are frowned upon, except at the beach or on the tennis court. Few people wear hats.

Working-class city dwellers usually wear inexpensive cotton clothes. The men are often seen in light-colored shirts open at the neck, paired with khaki pants, while the women wear print dresses, skirts, and blouses.

Children dress nicely for Mass on Sundays, as parents take pride in how their children look. Little girls often wear bright-colored ruffled dresses to Mass. Many of them have their ears pierced, and they wear gold jewelry. All children wear uniforms to school. In the poorest areas, some toddlers may walk around unclothed.

In rural areas, men often wear straw hats in hot weather and felt ones in cooler weather. Lower-class men often wear pants cut off at the knees and sandals. Some go barefoot. Upper-class men wear boots or shoes, but rarely dress in formal jackets and ties.

During the holidays in the lowlands, men wear traditional *liquiliqui* ("lih-kih-LIH-kih"), white cotton shirt and pants fastened with leather or

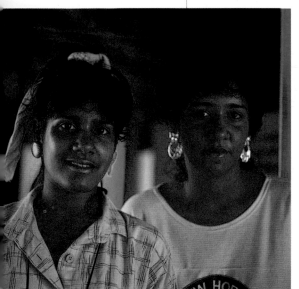

Above: **Venezuelans from Valencia dress in casual street wear.**

Opposite top: **A Guajiro Indian dresses sensibly, wearing black face paint to protect her complexion from salt and sun.**

Opposite bottom: **Hats and open-neck shirts are respectable attire at a Federation meeting.**

gold buttons or a sash. Women wear colorful full skirts called *joroperas* ("hoh-roh-PAY-rahs") with elaborately embroidered off-the-shoulder blouses.

While Guajiro men often dress in plain fashion, wearing only a shirt, loincloth, and straw hat, Guajiro women usually wear flowing, floor-length *mantas* ("MAHN-tahs") sewn in stunning colors. The Guajiros are also expert weavers of bright-colored saddlebags and belts.

LIFESTYLE

DESPITE EXTREME CONTRASTS in lifestyles across regions, there is a distinct Venezuelan personality and culture. The Venezuelan identity is shaped by the unique ways in which Venezuelans live, spend their days, and communicate.

GETTING BY OR LIVING IT UP?

Lifestyle variations in Venezuela are nowhere near as evident as in the living conditions in different regions. Venezuelans live in extremely different worlds: those who live in cities versus those who live in villages; those who live in houses or apartments versus those who live in shacks; those who are rich versus those who are poor.

Housing variations are particularly apparent in the big cities, especially Caracas, which suffers from an acute housing shortage. Periods of economic growth have drawn people to the capital in search of jobs. While many have found employment, few have found affordable housing.

Only the wealthiest *caraqueños* live in single-family homes, which are usually spacious, with a garden, swimming pool, and balcony. The house in Venezuela may not be the family's only property; the elite of Caracas often also have beach homes and apartments in North America.

Most of the middle and upper classes live in high-rise apartment buildings. The typical apartment is equipped with bedrooms, a kitchen, a bathroom, a living room, and a balcony. Many have servants' quarters, while the nicer buildings also have swimming pools.

Housing costs in Caracas are extremely high, comparable to those in New York, Tokyo, or Rio. Although the government has constructed some public housing in Caracas, demand still far exceeds supply. Hence, the poorest *caraqueños* have had to build shanties on the hilly outskirts of the city where they can live rent-free.

One in five Venezuelans lives in Caracas, and more than a third of caraqueños *live in slums.*

Opposite: **A Venezuelan boy hangs out with his donkey. Life in the rural areas differs greatly from life in the cities.**

Apartment blocks and shanties in Caracas. Some shanties are made from wooden planks and corrugated iron sheets. Waterproof shanties may have television sets and refrigerators powered by electricity tapped from transmission lines.

SPANISH ARCHITECTURE

Many Venezuelan homes have a distinctly Spanish look. Elegant houses built in colonial times have rooms built around a patio garden, a wall surrounding the house to guard the family's privacy, fancy iron gates and hardwood doors, bright-colored flowers in bloom hanging from a roof made from traditional dark-brown Spanish tiles, and walls painted in vibrant colors like lemon yellow, fuchsia, and emerald green.

RANCHOS

Ranchos, or shanties, are also found in the rural areas. The walls of rural *ranchos* are made from poles or bamboo, overlaid with palm fronds or mud. The roof is thatched with palm fronds, and the floor may be made from wooden planks (*right*). Kerosene lamps provide artificial light, and water is brought in from a nearby stream or well. Most of these homes have only two rooms: a kitchen and a living room or bedroom. Oil- or wood-burning stoves are used in the kitchen. Rooms can easily be added as the family grows. *Rancho* dwellers sleep in hammocks, or *chinchorros* ("chin-CHOR-rohs"), which are hung from large hooks in the walls. *Chinchorros* are comfortable and easy to store. The family may share the sleeping area with their pets and livestock such as chickens and goats.

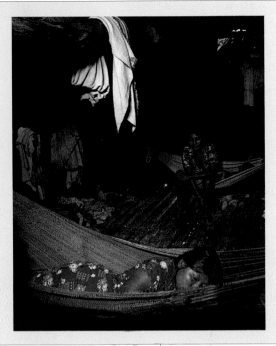

In many small towns in Venezuela, buildings and roads are arranged in a pattern that the Spanish colonists brought with them centuries ago. The town plan throughout the Spanish New World had government and religious buildings bordering the central plaza and streets laid out perpendicular to one another to give a sense of balance and harmony. The central plaza, which served as the marketplace, was flanked by the most important public buildings and the residences of the most influential citizens. The houses of government officials and businessmen stood just off the square. Townspeople in the lowest classes lived the farthest away from the plaza.

Left: **A bungalow in Caracas.**

63

THE FAMILY UNIT

In Venezuela, the family unit is more important than any of its individual members. Each member acknowledges and appreciates the essential role that every other member plays in the family. The children respect and revere their father as the head of the household and their mother as the manager of domestic affairs. Grandparents often form part of the household and are also treated with respect. Even when the children grow up, marry, and move away, they maintain close contact with their family and return home whenever they are needed.

A three-generation Venezuelan family.

In many Latin American cultures, the family circle is extended through the appointment of godparents: a *comadre* ("kom-MAH-dray"), or "co-mother", and a *compadre* ("kom-PAH-dray"), or "co-father." The godparents are supposed to ensure their godchildren's religious and moral education. Parents usually ask only close friends whom they trust and admire to be their children's godparents. Often, the godparents act as sponsors for their godchildren, contributing money to the First Communion ceremony, for instance, or helping their godchildren make connections when seeking employment later in life.

THE VENEZUELAN MAN AND THE LLANERO

The typical Venezuelan man has a traditional view of life. He is the chief—and often the sole—wage earner and makes all the family decisions. He prefers his wife not to work, as that would imply that he cannot provide adequately for the family. Venezuelan men are quite conscious of the image they present to society. They would never wish to appear weak or unmasculine or dominated by their wives.

The typical Venezuelan man regards the cowboy of the *llanos*, or the *llanero*, as a hero. The *llanero* does not exist only in Venezuelan folklore; he lives in the sparsely populated central region of the country, where the seasons alternate between flood and drought. The *llanero* is famed for his courage and strength. The legendary *llanero* drank nothing but a cup of strong coffee in the morning and spent his day on a half-wild horse, rounding up his herd with a lasso and driving the cattle to be branded. In the wet season, he followed his cattle in a canoe; in the dry season, he drove them across the plains in a cloud of heat and dust.

After an exhausting day, the *llanero* sat by the fire with his companions and talked about the events of the day over a hearty meal. Playing his *cuatro* ("KWAH-troh"), a four-stringed guitar, the *llanero* danced and sang about the suffering of his Indian ancestors. At the end of the day, he hung up his hammock to sleep and recharge for the next sunrise.

The llanero *leads a solitary existence. His motto is: "I, on my horse, above me my hat, above my hat, God." He is free and indomitable and lives by muscle and determination to battle nature.*

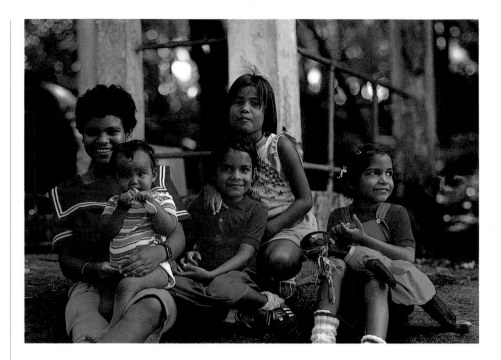

The traditional Venezuelan woman is a homemaker, and her family is her main concern.

THE VENEZUELAN WOMAN

Venezuelan women—like most Latin American women—tend to be conservative. Many Latin American women do not go out alone or even in groups at night unless accompanied by male companions such as their father or their brothers.

The typical Latin American woman is likely to dress conventionally. She may not assert her personality or put forth her ideas readily in public, but she does have considerable power within the home.

Most Latin American women hope to get married and raise children. Within the home, they see themselves as administrators overseeing the household budget, the housework, the children's religious upbringing, and the family's social activities. Children treat their mothers with unreserved affection; they are often not as openly affectionate with their fathers, the disciplinarians.

Wives and mothers are very concerned with cleanliness in the home and with personal hygiene. They bathe their children two or three times a day and dress them in freshly washed and pressed clothes for dinner.

WOMEN IN THE WORK FORCE

Economic development and urbanization have created employment opportunities for Venezuelan women. The female percentage of the country's work force has risen from less than 20 percent in 1950 to over 40 percent in the late 1990s. Fewer women are leaving the work force after marriage; more women between ages 35 and 44 are entering or staying in the work force.

Students in a chemistry laboratory at a university in Mérida. Women in the cities are taking on technical and professional careers.

More women have moved from rural areas to the cities and found a broader range of jobs open to them, including domestic and factory work. More women are entering professional and technical fields, building careers as doctors, lawyers, dentists, architects, teachers, nurses, laboratory technicians, and government officials. The 1989 presidential elections saw the country's first woman candidate, Ismenia Villaba. There are now 16 women in the 131-seat National Assembly. A former Miss Universe winner, Irene Sáez, was mayor of the Chacao district of Caracas before she became one of three main candidates for the presidency in 1998. She is now governor of the state of Nueva Esparta, which includes Margarita Island.

Women of the upper classes often devote themselves to charitable causes, supporting adult literacy programs and cultural institutions such as museums and ballet companies. It is prestigious for them to go to college, even if they have no intention of working after graduation. More than 50 percent of students enrolled in universities in Venezuela in 1990 were women.

Despite having achieved high levels of professional success and financial independence, many Venezuelan women still choose to promote their femininity and avoid appearing aggressive or competitive.

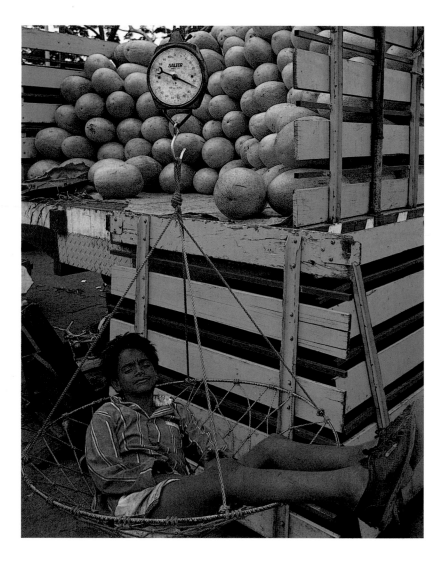

A Venezuelan boy takes a break at the marketplace in Ciudad Bolívar.

CHILDREN

Most Venezuelan babies and children are well cared for, whether they are born into upper- or lower-class families. Small children receive a lot of attention from all members of the extended family. Little girls are encouraged to be motherly toward their younger siblings and passive when interacting with boys their age. As children grow, girls are watched more closely than are their brothers, who are given fewer responsibilities and more freedom.

EDUCATION

In the past, only upper-class Venezuelans had access to formal education. School was thought to be unnecessary for middle- and lower-class children, who took manual jobs. Rómulo Betancourt's government, which took office in 1959, was the first to place emphasis on education. Educational material was brought in, teacher-training programs were developed, and some 2,287 new schools were built throughout the country in just five years.

Today, 90 percent of Venezuelan children attend school: 15 percent attend private, church-related primary and secondary schools; 75 percent go to schools directly administered by the ministry of education in Caracas. Public education from kindergarten through university is free. Some children in the most remote areas have only a one-room schoolhouse and an undertrained teacher to report to; some have no school to go to at all.

Primary school children in Venezuela study subjects similar to those that their counterparts in the United States study. These include reading, writing, arithmetic, natural science, history, geography, and civics.

After six years of primary school, students attend a four-year program in science and the humanities. A second program including philosophy, literature, physical science, mathematics, and biology prepares them for college. Secondary school students can attend technical schools for instruction in industry, commerce, nursing, and social welfare.

About 450 Venezuelan students are enrolled in university programs. Most of them study economics, business, law, health, and engineering. Leading public universities include the Central University of Venezuela founded in 1725, the Los Andes University, and the Simón Bolívar University. The government also administers extensive adult literacy and job-training programs.

Total school enrolment in 1958 was 845,000; by 1989, it was nearly three million. The literacy rate, which was just over 50 percent in the 1950s, reached 82 percent by the 1970s and 91.1 percent in 2000.

Thank-you notes are expected after a show of courtesy, and many Venezuelans send flowers after having dinner at the home of a friend or business associate.

SOCIAL GRACES

The big Venezuelan cities have become more internationally oriented since the oil boom and the influx of foreigners. The United States in particular has made a significant impact on Venezuelan society, but not so much that Venezuelans—especially those of the upper classes—have given up their social rituals.

Venezuelan society is essentially hierarchical. Rank is very important. Older people come before younger people; people with titles wield more influence than those without; members of the upper class may be served in a restaurant before middle-class diners who arrived first. When someone holds a title such as doctor or professor, it is important to use it when addressing him or her.

Receiving an invitation to a Venezuelan home is considered something of an honor. The home is a refuge, a place where only the extended family and closest friends are welcome. Guests who fall into neither of these categories are treated formally. In a small party, the guest is introduced by the host or hostess and is expected to greet, shake hands with, and say goodbye to each of the other guests individually. At large gatherings, the guests introduce themselves to one another. The casual "hi, everybody" and "take care" that Americans arrive and leave with would be considered undignified at a Venezuelan gathering.

Certain subjects of conversation are taboo at dinner parties, especially for foreigners. It is considered impolite to gossip or spread rumors about well-known personalities, to discuss politics, to tell political jokes, or to talk about the problem of illegal aliens from Colombia. Controversial subjects are not raised, as arguing must be avoided at all costs. Venezuelans do not like being asked personal questions about marriage or family, for instance, until they know the person fairly well.

Venezuelans make social calls to admire a new baby or house or to thank a host or hostess for dinner. However, they do not visit between 1 and 4 P.M., as the siesta hours are a time to nap, read, or write letters. In the United States, neighbors often drop in on a newcomer to welcome him or her to the area. In Venezuela, it is just the opposite. Newcomers call on the established members of the community to introduce themselves.

In Venezuela, a cup of coffee is the symbol of hospitality. It is offered during a social call, after dinner, or at the start of a business meeting. It is considered rude to decline a cup of coffee, but it is acceptable to drink only one or two sips. There are two rules when the bill arrives after a meal: the person who made the invitation pays for everyone; and the man never lets the woman pay.

A sidewalk café in Caracas. Venezuelans are more likely to entertain someone they know only casually at a club or restaurant.

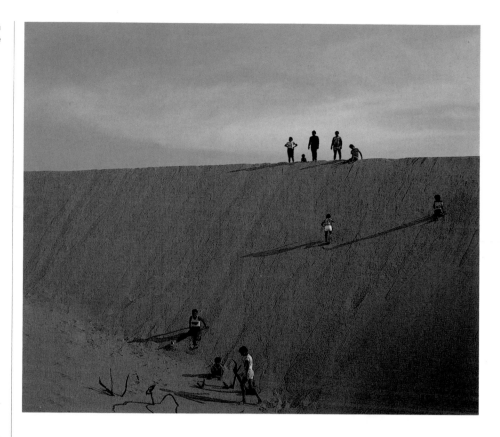

TAKING TIME

Venezuelans like to take their time. If they arrive late for an appointment, it may be because they were taking time to be courteous at a previous meeting. Venezuelans have a relaxed attitude toward tardiness. In Caracas, where traffic jams are common, delays are considered a part of life, and *caraqueños* accept them casually, even cheerfully. When entering an office or shop, it is more important to stop and greet the receptionist or shopkeeper than to rush about accomplishing something. A smile or nod is all that is required.

In business, Venezuelans take their time to assess a situation before offering an idea or making a decision. Personal relationships also progress slowly and carefully. Venezuelans are not likely to appreciate an impatient businessperson who demands an immediate answer or an acquaintance who asks intimate questions.

THE LIFE CYCLE

Most significant life events in Venezuela are outwardly similar to those in other countries where the main religion is Roman Catholicism. There are some differences, however, in the way Venezuelans celebrate birthdays, coming-of-age events, weddings, and funerals, which give meaningful insights into their cultural identity.

BIRTH The birth of a child is a time of great rejoicing. Relatives and close family friends flock to the home of the newborn to celebrate the arrival. Traditionally, older people bring a strong homemade liquor to toast the baby's health.

In general, boys are preferred, since they are easier to bring up than girls. For instance, there is no need to chaperone a boy when he goes out. Upper-class Venezuelans often choose to have big families with eight or nine children. Poor families sometimes have even more. Most middle-class couples are well informed about family planning and opt for a small family with only two or three children.

In 1992, Venezuela's birth rate was 27 in 1,000; in 2000, it was 21 in 1,000. This is still a high birth rate, even though fewer babies are being born.

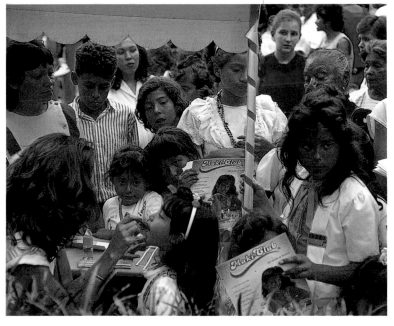

Venezuelan girls learn to put on makeup. They are introduced to the art of femininity at an early age.

All eyes are turned in anticipation on the *piñata*.

BIRTHDAYS Venezuelans throw parties to celebrate their children's birthday. The highlight of children's birthday parties is often the *piñata* ("pih-NYAH-tah"), a bright-colored figure in the shape of a man or animal that is stuffed with toys and candy. Blindfolded, all the children at the party take turns trying to hit the *piñata* with a stick until it breaks open releasing its contents. There are entire shops in Venezuela selling nothing but *piñatas* and toys and candy to put in them.

THE 15TH BIRTHDAY When Venezuelan girls reach the age of 15, many have a *quinceañera* ("kin-say-ah-nee-AIR-ah"), a special 15th birthday party. This ritual, a Latin form of the debutante or "coming out" party, is common in many South American cultures. It announces to society that the girl is now a woman and is ready to join the social world. In the past, the purpose of the *quinceañera* was to bring the girl into contact with eligible men, but this has become an obsolete function in modern South American countries, where boys and girls interact in social situations from an early age. The scale of expenses varies: poorer families may invite a hundred or so guests, while wealthy families have been known to invite thousands.

Most parties are held in a club or hall. For wealthy families, the party is usually held at home. The larger celebrations can cost a great deal and can put the family in debt for years.

The party begins at about 9 P.M, and can last until dawn, but usually ends at about 2 A.M. Dinner and drinks are served, although the birthday girl is usually only allowed a sip of champagne from her father's glass. For dessert, there is usually a large cake. In wealthy families, it is multi-tiered like a wedding cake.

Girls and women often wear fancy ball gowns, and boys and men wear either nice suits or tuxedos. There is often a band, and the birthday girl traditionally dances the first dance, which is likely to be a waltz, with her father. Then she dances with her male peers. It is considered a status symbol to give a fancy *quinceañera*. In the big cities, the party will often be covered in the newspapers.

WEDDINGS Wedding parties are often grand affairs. Like *quinceañeras*, weddings are an opportunity to invite many guests and to show society that no expense is spared in celebrating a milestone in the life of a daughter. Among the upper classes, it is considered good luck if the bride and groom can sneak away from the wedding celebration within a few hours of its commencement without being noticed.

FUNERALS Funerals are solemn occasions. Often, after the ceremony, family members gather at the home of the departed to comfort the family. The wife of a deceased man usually wears black for a long time, if she is a religious woman. Some widows even wear black for the rest of their lives. Less traditional or younger widows are not likely to wear black at all. Widowers often wear dark clothes for a week or month.

Many Venezuelan customs and attitudes can be traced back to the colonial period.

RELIGION

THE OFFICIAL RELIGION of Venezuela is Roman Catholicism, though the constitution guarantees freedom of religion. In 2000, 96 percent of Venezuelans were Catholic, 2 percent Protestant, and the remaining 2 percent followers of other religions.

The Spanish brought Catholicism to Venezuela. In 1513, Dominican and Franciscan priests came to northeastern Venezuela to develop coffee, sugar, and cocoa plantations and to teach indigenous Indians cattle breeding. Capuchin missionaries founded 100 stations in the *llanos* between 1658 and 1758, while Jesuits were active in the Orinoco River areas. They were quite successful in converting the locals and in building and running religious schools throughout the country.

Although the Church in Venezuela is not formally linked to the State, it does receive financial support from the government in the form of salaries for some church officials and subsidies for church building maintenance. The Church also consults the government when naming powerful church officials, and church representatives often attend important secular functions, such as the opening of a power plant.

Venezuela has many beautiful Catholic churches; there is at least one in each town. Many are modeled after the Cathedral of Coro on the Caribbean coast and La Asuncíon on Margarita Island, both completed in 1617. Architectural ornamentation is minimal.

Opposite: **The Sanctuary of Our Lady of El Valle on Margarita Island.**

Above: **Vendors wait for customers outside the Cathedral of Mérida.**

Opposite: **The wooden pews and tiled floor of San Francisco's church, near Maracaibo, are typical features of churches in Venezuela.**

CATHOLIC BELIEFS AND TRADITIONS

Roman Catholics believe that the pope is the supreme leader of the Church. According to Catholic tradition, the present-day pope is the latest in a succession of popes starting with Saint Peter, who was appointed by Jesus Christ as the cornerstone of the Church. The pope is believed to be infallible in making decisions on matters of the faith. Roman Catholics receive six of seven sacraments, or signs of grace, to develop spiritually.

BAPTISM A baby is baptized to be cleansed of "original sin," or sin inherited from the disobedience of Adam and Eve, the father and mother of the human race, according to Christian beliefs. Baptism gives each newborn a fresh start in life and allows it to become a member of the Church. This sacrament is performed by a priest, who pours water over the baby's forehead while saying, "I baptize you in the name of the Father and of the Son and of the Holy Spirit."

Baptism marks a milestone in the life of every individual entering the Catholic faith, regardless of social class. Venezuelans living in remote areas of the country, away from parish centers, travel long distances to have their babies baptized. Poorer parents may have to wait until they can raise enough money for a proper christening party or choose godparents who are willing and able to contribute money. In wealthier families, christening parties can be elaborate affairs.

CONFIRMATION Catholics are usually confirmed between the ages of 12 and 18. Confirmation is the sacrament that seals the faith received at baptism. It indicates that the person is now an adult and is responsible for his or her own religious life. Confirmed Catholics have a duty to live out their faith through prayer and acts of charity.

HOLY EUCHARIST Also called Holy Communion, this sacrament serves as a channel for spiritual nourishment. Catholics believe that Jesus Christ exists in the bread and wine consecrated on the altar at every Mass. The first part of the Mass consists of readings from the scriptures; the second part focuses on the Holy Eucharist. When Catholics ingest the bread and wine, they believe they receive the body and blood of Christ, the source of life. Before receiving the sacrament, they are expected to meditate and pray and to have fasted for an hour before the Mass.

Catholic children make their First Holy Communion at about the age of 7, when they are considered to know the difference between right and wrong.

PENANCE This sacrament entails the confession of sins. A confessor enters a box-like cubicle inside the church and reveals to a priest, who represents God, the sins he or she has committed. The priest then forgives the confessor in the name of God and assigns the confessor a penance: the recitation of certain prayers or performance of a ritual to atone for the sins confessed.

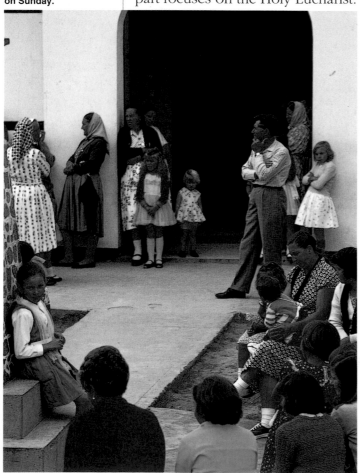

Worshipers congregate outside a church before Mass. Catholics attend Mass at least once a week, on Sunday.

MATRIMONY Among Catholics, marriage is a sacred bond that unites a couple and allows them to have children. Catholic marriages should not be broken by divorce, although divorce does happen in Venezuela, as in many countries.

ANOINTING OF THE SICK This sacrament is performed on the very sick and the dying. Also known as "last rites," the anointing of the sick brings forgiveness to the dying and prepares them for entry into heaven. The priest applies olive oil—symbolic of light, strength, and life— on the forehead of the recipient and asks for God's forgiveness of all sins committed by the person through sight, touch, taste, smell, and hearing.

In the church grounds in the German immigrant settlement of Colonia Tovar.

HOLY ORDERS This sacrament applies only to priests. It is performed by a bishop, who lays his hands on the candidate for priesthood and gives him the power to minister the other sacraments, such as Holy Eucharist and Holy Matrimony. Only men can become priests in the Catholic Church; they take a vow of celibacy, promising to never marry. There are several grades of priestly vocation: a monsignor performs special duties in a Catholic community; a bishop takes care of a diocese, the Catholic community in a city; an archbishop serves a large city; and a cardinal is an archbishop appointed by the pope as an adviser. One of the most significant functions of cardinals is to elect a new pope.

Interior of Barquisimeto Cathedral, designed by Jan Berg Kemp.

ATTITUDES TOWARD CATHOLICISM

Although most Venezuelans consider themselves Catholic, religion does not play a significant role in daily life for all of them. Of the entire population, 96 percent are nominally Catholic, but only 25 percent practise their faith. Generally, only the elderly attend Mass daily and pray before meals. Most of the younger Catholics attend Mass only on festive religious occasions such as Christmas, weddings, baptisms, and saints' days. For them, the social atmosphere often takes precedence over the religious significance of the ceremony.

The women tend to be more religious than the men, perhaps because they are responsible for the moral and religious education of their children. Boys are generally not encouraged to enter the religious life, as devotion is not considered a masculine trait. This may be why the Church has difficulty recruiting Venezuelan priests. Although about half the nuns in the country are local women, most priests in Venezuela come from Spain. Venezuelan priests usually come from the middle class, which has historically been more religious than the other classes.

Catholics in the rural states of Mérida, Táchira, and Trujillo, where agricultural traditions have been maintained, tend to be more devoted to

THE CULT OF MARÍA LIONZA

María Lionza is the goddess of nature and fertility, and protector of forests, wild animals, and mineral wealth. She is worshiped by cult groups from all social classes in Venezuela, although she is particularly popular among the urban poor. The cult of María Lionza originated from Indian, African, and Christian beliefs and practices. She has characteristics of the Arawak water goddess, West African mythological figures, and the Virgin Mary.

Legend has it that María Lionza was a beautiful Indian girl, who disappeared in the forest and was never seen again, except as a spirit. She is said to live with her servants in a golden palace surrounded by wild animals in the Sorte Mountains of Yaracuy. She rides on the back of a tapir, a gentle beast considered sacred by some Indian groups.

During cult services, a priest calls up spirits, and the spirits possess mediums. The spirits are consulted for advice and assistance. Tobacco smoke is used as a cure, to ward off evil spirits, and to bring about spiritual cleansing.

María Lionza has been associated with popular Catholic saints, with a historical figure named Negro Miguel who instigated an uprising among the slaves, and even with Simón Bolívar, the Venezuelan liberator. In the Sorte Mountains, there are countless images of the goddess. In ceremonies that take place in the mountains, candles burn everywhere and worshipers often go barefoot to maintain physical contact with the earth. They never stand with arms or hands crossed, as this is said to bring bad luck.

The worship of María Lionza takes many different forms throughout the country. An attempt was made to unify cult groups in 1968, when they were legalized as a society under the name of the Aboriginal Cult of María Lionza, with its headquarters in Caracas.

their faith than Catholics in the cities. Perhaps the stresses of urban life leave little time for spiritual affairs; and perhaps the lure of the material world distracts sophisticated city folk from thoughts of life after death.

FOLK BELIEFS AND SUPERSTITIONS

Folk beliefs based on the occult are common throughout Venezuela, especially in remote rural areas. Folk beliefs combine Catholic beliefs and practices with those of African and Indian faiths. In the Andes, some people believe that physical objects like water contain supernatural powers. Venezuelans of all ethnic origins seek the advice of resident faith healers. Many indigenous Indians, especially among the Arawak and Carib, believe in the power of spiritualists.

Venezuelans are generally a superstitious people. Many believe in witches and demons that take on human form and other spirits that take on animal forms. *Anima solas* ("ah-NEE-mah SOH-lahs"), or "lost souls," are said to make occasional appearances, and it is believed they are best diffused by covering one's face and praying aloud.

In Venezuela, it is Tuesday the 13th rather than Friday the 13th that is considered unlucky. North American superstitions about walking under ladders and letting black cats cross your path are also heeded by Venezuelans. For good luck a polished seed of a tropical tree is as good as a rabbit's foot. The seed can be given as a gift, stolen, or found, but it must never be bought.

Some Venezuelans consider it bad luck to receive a handkerchief, seashell, live snake, or anything made from snakeskin. Others consider a rattlesnake tail to be a symbol of good luck. If the palm of your right hand itches, then someone owes you money; if the itch is in the left hand, then *you* owe someone money. When you open a bottle of rum, you are supposed to spill a few drops on the ground in order to give the dead a taste. In Venezuela, if you dream about a snake, it means that someone is gossiping about you; if in the dream you behead the snake, that indicates that you have stopped the gossip from spreading.

Catholics ask Saint Anthony for help when they are in need of special favors. Folk believers in rural Venezuela tie down a small statue of Saint Anthony until he grants them their request.

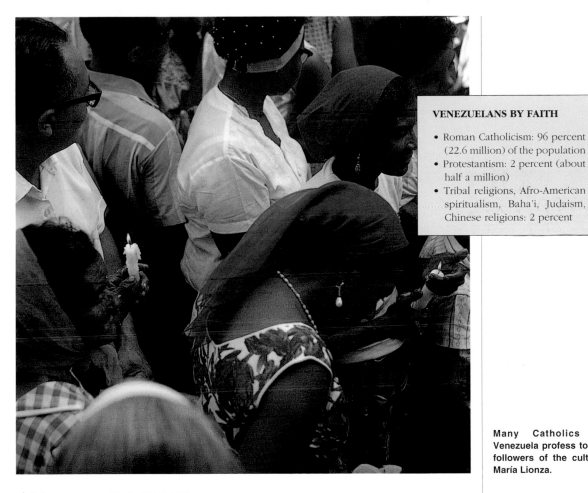

VENEZUELANS BY FAITH

- Roman Catholicism: 96 percent (22.6 million) of the population
- Protestantism: 2 percent (about half a million)
- Tribal religions, Afro-American spiritualism, Baha'i, Judaism, Chinese religions: 2 percent

Many Catholics in Venezuela profess to be followers of the cult of María Lionza.

OTHER RELIGIONS

The Baha'i and Protestant faiths have experienced rapid growth in Venezuela in recent years, converting many Guajiro Indians. Judaism is represented in Venezuela by both Sephardic groups that came from Spain and Ashkenazi groups that emigrated from central and eastern Europe after World War II.

Islam came to Venezuela first with African slaves and later with waves of migrants from India and Pakistan (end of the 16th century), then Syria and Lebanon (middle of the 19th century).

There are also several Greek and Ukrainian Orthodox congregations in Venezuela, as well as followers of Buddhism.

GALERIAS 1.890
SU CENTRO COMERCIAL

El Regalo Dorado

LA MODA
Kuroki
DEL JAPO

...uno
BOUTIQUE

Fantasías Nathalí
BROCHES-ZARCILLOS-COLLARES
ELABORACION - MATERIALES
CURSO

CUR os ARTE
Artesanía

Tia Nicota

Salón de t
Dulcería
Bombonerí

HUDU

FOTOCOPIAS
TRANSCRIPCION DE TEXTOS Lo

Génesis
DISEÑOS

Cristeras REGALO

LANGUAGE

THE OFFICIAL LANGUAGE of Venezuela is Spanish, the language of the *conquistadores*. The standard of Spanish among educated Venezuelans is uniform throughout the country, but the standard varies from region to region among the less educated.

People from the Andean states of Mérida, Trujillo, and Táchira speak with a refined accent. In Maracaibo, people accentuate their syllables clearly, while inhabitants of Cumaná and Margarita Island speak fast. The *llaneros* have a distinct accent, as do the inhabitants of Coro and Caracas. Nevertheless, everyone understands everyone else.

"VENEZUELANISMS"

People of all classes and ethnic groups are familiar with many distinctly Venezuelan words. Some of these words come from several African and Indian languages, while others have Spanish origins.

Indian words that have found their way into the Venezuelan vocabulary include the Cumanagoto-derived *butaca* ("boo-TAH-kah"), meaning theater stall, and the Arawak-derived *hamaca* ("ah-MAH-kah"), meaning hammock, *barbacoa* ("bar-bah-KOH-ah"), meaning barbecue, and *tabaco* ("ta-BAH-koh"), meaning tobacco. Some of these words were eventually Anglicized as well.

Opposite: **Despite the pervasive influence of English, shop signs are all in Spanish.**

Below: **A signboard in Venezuelan Spanish.**

MADE IN VENEZUELA

Some English words used in Venezuela may have different pronunciations and even different meanings. In Venezuela, "okay" can mean the same thing it means in English-speaking cultures, or it can mean "goodbye." And if you say "yes" or "yeah" to a Venezuelan, he or she will probably not understand you.

Here are a few distinctly Venezuelan words and phrases; some hint at the jovial, light-hearted personality of the Venezuelan people.

GORDO or *GORDA* ("GOR-doh" or "GOR-dah") literally means "fat," but is used as a term of affection, not to be taken as an offense.

TELECULEBRA ("tay-lay-koo-LAY-brah") literally means "television snake," but is used to describe a soap opera in which the characters are greedy, lustful, or cunning.

MAS O MENOS ("mass oh MAY-noss") translates as "more or less" and may be an answer to "How are you?" ("Okay, not great") or "How much did it cost?" ("Not too much, not too little").

CHEVERE ("chair-BAY-ray") is the equivalent of "wow" or "great."

QUE PALO DE AGUA! ("kay PAH-loh day AH-guah") literally means "What a stick of water!" but is used to mean "What a rainstorm!"

QUE GANGA! ("kay GAHNG-gah") translates as "What a bargain!" It may be heard in shops.

Some "Venezuelanisms" of Spanish origin have been adapted for use in modern situations. For example, in Caracas, a city renowned for traffic jams, *caraqueños* have devised a vocabulary to describe various types of congestion: a *galletas* ("gah-YEH-taz") is your average traffic jam; *colas* ("KOH-lahs") are long lines of traffic that crawl at snail's pace; and a *tranca* ("TRAHN-cah") is a complete roadblock. *Vivos* ("BEE-bohs") are drivers who pay no attention to traffic laws and thus often cause accidents.

AMERICAN INFLUENCE

Venezuelans who travel regularly or who come in contact with people from other cultures speak English as well as other languages, such as Portuguese, French, German, and Italian. There are also substantial immigrant populations whose first language is Portuguese or Italian.

English has been creeping steadily into the language, especially in urban areas, because of the influx of North Americans employed in the petroleum industry. In the areas of sports and recreation, the influence of the *yanqui* ("JAN-kee"), or yankee, is clear. For instance, in the national sport of baseball, called *beisbol* ("beh-EES-bol") in Venezuela, "ball one" is *bol uán* ("bol OO-wan"), "ball two" is *bol tu* ("bol TOO"), "strike three" is *estrai tri* ("ess-TRAH-ee tree"), "struck out" is *estrocao* ("ess-troh-KAH-oh"), "hit" is *hit* ("heet"), and "home run" is *jonrón* ("khon-RHON"). If these terms were translated directly into Spanish, they would not sound nearly as American.

Other Americanisms have been adopted in the office and beyond, such as "all right," or *olrai* ("OHL-rah-ee"). A security guard or night watchman is called a *wachiman* ("wah-chih-MAHN"), a clutch in a standard shift car is a *croche* ("CROH-chay"), and when your gas tank reads "F," it is, in short, *full* ("fool").

Tourists in a hotel on the Caribbean coast. A working knowledge of English is an asset in the service industries, particularly those related to tourism. However, many linguistic purists in Venezuela object to the importation of foreign words. Despite a law that requires all foreign advertising copy to be translated completely into Spanish, English words continue to assault the Venezuelan vocabulary.

Teachers in Caracas demonstrate for the literacy campaign.

A UNIFYING FORCE

Most Venezuelans speak only Spanish. This common language serves as a unifying base, contributing to the *Venezolano* sense of identity. Although there are distinct words to define the different ethnic groups, these terms do not carry racist connotations. A *blanco* ("BLAHN-koh") is simply a Caucasian, a *negro* ("NAY-groh") an African, a *mulatto* ("moo-LAHT-toh") an African–Caucasian mix, a *pardo* ("PAR-doh") someone of African, Caucasian, and Indian heritage, and a *zambo* ("ZAHM-boh") an Indian–African mix. A *mestizo*, which used to mean someone of Indian and European heritage, has come to designate all ethnic permutations.

INDIAN LANGUAGES

Before the *conquistadores* found Venezuela, the country was inhabited by culturally diverse groups of Indians. Historians speculate that there were four related groups of Indian languages in Venezuela before the Spanish arrived. These language groups were Cariban, Arawakan, Paezan, and Chibchan. Many indigenous peoples in Venezuela—and their ancient languages—became extinct during the Spanish conquest. Linguists believe that just about 100 different languages and dialects are today spoken by Indians in Venezuela.

SPANISH NAMES

Many Venezuelans of Spanish heritage have double last names that can be confusing. If a man's name is Pedro Jimenez Garcia, he is called Señor Jimenez. Jimenez is his father's surname, and Garcia is his mother's maiden name. The latter distinguishes him from his cousins, who might be Emilio Jimenez Martinez or Jaime Jimenez Rodriquez.

Guajiros speak their own language, but assimilation into mainstream society has encouraged them to also speak Spanish.

If Pedro Jimenez Garcia marries Maria Estrada Gonzales, she becomes Maria Estrada de Jimenez or Señora de Jimenez. Estrada was her father's name and Gonzales her mother's maiden name, which is now dropped. Their children's surname will be Jimenez Estrada.

ADDRESSES AND STREET NAMES IN CARACAS

Downtown Caracas is laid out on a grid, with streets running either parallel to or at right angles with a main north–south street. Parallel streets are identified by numbers, while streets laid out in an east–west direction have names. Many addresses are stated as intersections. For example, Hoyo a Santa Rosalía designates the intersection of Hoyo and Santa Rosalía streets.

Corners derive their names from nearby buildings, well-known people who lived on them, or events that took place on them. For example, in Plaza Bolívar, the southeastern corner is called *Las Gradillas*, or "The Stairs," because at one time, a flight of steps led into the square at that spot. On the south side is a corner called *Las Monjas,* or "The Nuns," a name derived from an 18th-century convent that used to stand there. The convent was said to have been founded by a rich woman who encouraged the female members of her family to become nuns. There were once 70 nuns living in the convent. The building was demolished in 1874.

Caracas has five corners named after *La Virgen del Carmen*, or Our Lady of Mount Carmel. The best-known of these, near Plaza Miranda, is called *El Carmen*, because of an image of the Virgin Mary carved in relief on the facade of a building that once stood there.

There are many other examples of street corners named in similar fashion: one is called *Pelota* after a game that was once played there; another is called *Hospital* for a hospital that once stood there. The Marquis of Mijares lived on the corner called *Mijares*, and the street corner *Diaz* is named for a Dr. Diaz.

NOTIONS OF SPACE

Venezuelans, like other Latin Americans, are warm, demonstrative people: they tend to communicate a lot through body language and stand close to one another when conversing. While North Americans typically stand around 20 inches (51 cm) apart, Latin Americans keep a much smaller distance between themselves. This may make many North Americans feel uncomfortable, but it is considered unfriendly or cold to back away.

At formal meetings, Venezuelans do not like facing each other across a table. Foreigners working in Venezuela are thus urged to furnish their offices with a sofa, or comfortable chairs placed arm to arm, so that participants in a business discussion can sit next to each other. Talking across a table can make Venezuelans feel uncomfortable or even snubbed.

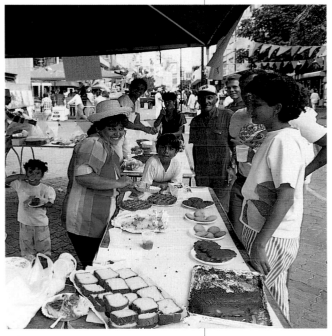

Eye contact and a warm manner speak volumes when Venezuelans converse.

Venezuelans tend to touch each other often. When introduced, two people shake hands. By the second meeting, new acquaintances are likely to embrace or pat each other on the right shoulder. This custom, the *abrazo* ("ah-BRAH-soh"), is done by both men and women. The shoulder pat is also used to comfort another person or when enjoying a good joke. Men and women who are good friends kiss each other to say hello and goodbye, as do women friends. Women often walk arm-in-arm in public.

At a party, it is important to shake hands with each guest upon arriving and before leaving, and to look a person in the eye when speaking.

ARTS

VENEZUELANS HAVE A LONG HISTORY of achievements in poetry, music, painting, and oratory. They are also well-known for their Indian pottery, basketry, and weaving.

Caracas is the cultural and artistic center of the country. It is the home of museums and art galleries, including the Museo de Arte Contemporáneo (Museum of Contemporary Art), Galería de Arte Nacional (National Art Gallery), and Museo de Bellas Artes (Museum of Fine Arts), which specialize in works by both Venezuelan and foreign artists. The Venezuelan Symphony Orchestra offers concerts ranging from the classical to the modern; it even plays occasionally at subway stations during the rush hour as part of the Metro's cultural program. Caracas has an accomplished ballet troupe, a national opera company, and several smaller musical ensembles. Architecturally, the city has earned a reputation for innovation and imagination, especially through the buildings designed by the country's most famous architect, Carlos Raúl Villanueva.

Above: **At Casa Natal, the birthplace of Simón Bolívar, visitors can see the family bed and Bolívar's library and files.**

Opposite: **Gente XX**, **a sculpture in various materials, including wood and polychrome. It was executed by Gaudi Este in 1982 and is displayed in the Museo de Bellas Artes, Caracas.**

Colonial homes have been painstakingly restored. The Museo de Arte Colonial (Museum of Colonial Art), a splendid 18th-century country residence, provides a glimpse of the lifestyle of a wealthy colonial family. In Spanish tradition, the main house is surrounded by walls and encloses a patio. The rooms are filled with period furniture, paintings, and religious artifacts, and the balconies look out over a garden filled with indigenous orchids. A bathroom in a separate building has a large stone tub into which fresh spring water used to run. Kitchens, storerooms, and stables have been stocked with period utensils, tools, and carriages.

The Catholic influence is apparent in the churches of Venezuela. Above is the Chapel of Santo Domingo.

CULTURAL HISTORY

During the colonial period, it was the Catholic Church that was primarily responsible for encouraging cultural development. Venezuela's scholars and intellectuals were educated in religious schools, and their thoughts and writings reflected their religious background. At the same time, the Church was also a great patron of the visual arts: it commissioned paintings and sculptures of religious events and figures for the numerous churches and cathedrals in the country.

In the 18th century, the first portrait paintings began to appear in Venezuela, and in about 1784, the first plays were produced in Caracas' first theater. During the last years of the colonial era, the country was known throughout the Spanish empire for the brilliance of its composers and musicians.

Simón Bolívar was the leading intellectual of the independence movement. He had extraordinary oratorical abilities and his literary work is still considered to be among the country's finest prose. His tutor, Andrés Bello, a poet and philosopher, wrote the first book ever printed in Venezuela. He left the country with Bolívar in 1810 and eventually settled in Chile, where he helped develop the national education system.

During the independence era, painting became increasingly important, as subject matter turned toward the political and historical. Juan Lovera, a self-taught artist, is famous for his group portraits of the leaders of the movement. After independence, artists rejected the Church's cultural hold

A bronze sculpture, *La Tempestad*, by Lorenzo Gonzalez, in the Museum of Fine Arts.

and turned to events of the immediate past for inspiration, although they kept their European roots in terms of style. Poets such as José Antonio Martin and Abigaíl Lozano were popular during this time, as was Fermin Toro, who wrote some of Venezuela's first novels.

From 1870 to 1888, during the reign of the dictator Antonio Guzmán Blanco, Venezuela became culturally more sophisticated. A great admirer and patron of the arts, Guzmán Blanco built the Municipal Theater and the first Academy of Fine Arts and appointed French romantic painter, Martín Tovar y Tovar, later known as the "master of Venezuelan mural painting," as his official artist. Tovar y Tovar's follower, Arturo Michelena, became one of South America's best-known painters.

The Maracay bull ring built by President Juan Vicente Gómez was designed by Carlos Raúl Villanueva. It was the latter's first design project.

A dictator, Juan Vicente Gómez, who ruled Venezuela from 1908 to 1935, despised artists and intellectuals, and his reign inspired some of the country's finest political protest writing. Short story writer Rufino Blanco Fombona was known for his satiric attacks on Gómez and his followers.

Other early 20th-century writers who helped define the Venezuelan artistic style include Teresa de las Parra, an upper-class woman who wrote an intimate novel about the effects of industrialization on the life of a *criollo* woman. Romantic poetry written in traditional Spanish couplets was also popular during this period. The leader of the cultural movement, Andrés Eloy Blanco, was known for his lighthearted style and his use of well-known Venezuelan proverbs and myths.

One of Venezuela's leading painters during the early 20th century was Armando Reverón. He spent much of his life in the small coastal town of Macuto, where he took advantage of the sunny Caribbean climate to depict selected models and landscapes. For example, he created perhaps more than a hundred paintings of a small bay by his house, trying to capture the different shades of light produced at different times of the day.

RÓMULO GALLEGOS AND *DOÑA BÁRBARA*

Venezuela's most famous novel, published in 1929, is *Doña Bárbara* by Rómulo Gallegos. Translated into many languages, the novel is considered the finest example of what is known as *criollo* literature, work that is truly Venezuelan in theme and tone. Like much of Gallegos' work, *Doña Bárbara* addresses the theme of the intellectual who struggles to civilize corrupt and violent elements in Venezuelan society.

The book's hero, Santo Luzardo, represents the civilizing force; Doña Bárbara, the primary female character, represents the barbaric force. The novel is set on the *llanos*, described as "a wide and stretching land, all horizons like hope, all roads like the will."

Doña Bárbara is the beautiful and imperious leader of the *llaneros*. In her youth, her fiancé was killed and she was raped by a group of adventurers. From that point on, she despised men and vowed to dominate them. Now at the height of her power, she wields control over all the men of the *llanos*—peons, butlers, landowners, and judges. She is skillful with both knife and gun and orders assassinations without a thought.

In the end, however, Santo Luzardo overcomes Doña Bárbara and her followers with the help of working-class *llaneros*. The moral of the story: good always triumphs over evil.

Doña Bárbara brought Gallegos literary fame. The successful author later became a well-known politician. He served as director of the ministry of education in Caracas and became a member of both the senate and the house of deputies. In 1947, Gallegos was elected president, but was ousted by a military faction after only a few months in office. He died in 1969 at the age of 85.

Doña Bárbara was first made into a movie in 1943. Fernando de Fuentes wrote the screenplay and produced and directed his adaptation of Gallegos' novel. Then in 1999, Betty Kaplan made her same-titled epic with a cast from Spain, Argentina, Cuba, and the United States.

MODERN TRENDS

With democracy and economic prosperity following the oil boom, public interest in art increased substantially. The government began assigning funds to ambitious artistic establishments such as the national symphony and filmmaking and ballet companies. Venezuelan artists were exposed to the work of artists from other cultures, especially Europe and the United States, and this had a significant impact on local art. At the same time, interest in indigenous folk art revived.

LITERATURE Historical fiction continues to appeal to many Venezuelans. Home-grown authors such as Arturo Uslar Pietri and Miguel Otero Silva have written greatly admired novels about the Spanish conquest and 20th-century dictators in Venezuela. In 1980, Luis Brito García won great acclaim with *Abrapalabra*, an experimental historical novel that was awarded a coveted literary prize. The average young Venezuelan prefers the novels of Francisco Herrera Luque, which give simpler, more colorful accounts of recent historical events. His *Boves el Urogallo*, about the war of independence, sold more copies than any other novel in Venezuelan history.

A costumed performer joins the audience.

DANCE, MUSIC, THEATER In 1974, the national ballet company was established with dancers from all over the world. Ballet International de Caracas toured Latin America and the United States in the late 1970s, performing the national dance, the *joropo* ("ho-ROW-pow"), to music provided by renowned Venezuelan pianist Teresa Carreño.

Venezuela's established musical groups—including the Maracaibo Symphony Orchestra founded in the early 1970s, the Caracas Opera Company, and the Venezuelan Symphony Orchestra—have attained international recognition. Amateur and professional opera companies, choruses, and children's musical groups are popular locally.

In 2001, Caracas hosted its fifth Fiesta Internacional del Teatro San Martin, an annual international festival that brings together professional, amateur, and alternative theater groups.

PAINTING AND SCULPTURE Venezuelan painters and sculptors have attracted attention in the international art world. The work of painter and sculptor Jesús Raphael Soto, in particular, is widely collected and displayed. Soto has held major exhibitions at the Hirshhorn Gallery in

A music teacher leads a children's choir in an open-air rehearsal in Trujillo.

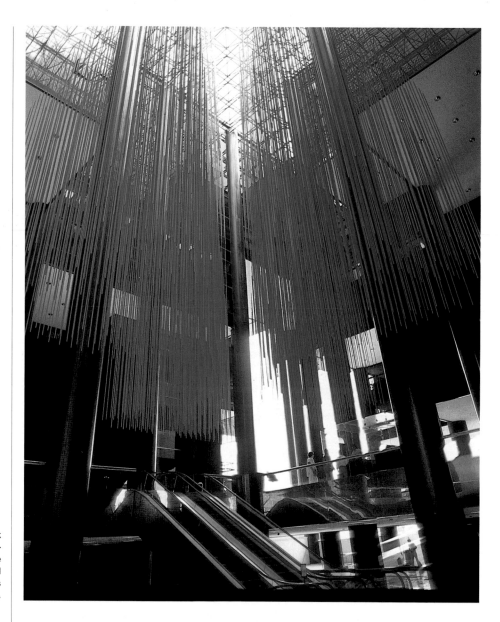

The interior of the "Black Cube" building in Caracas. Soto's creations are multi-dimensional and use a variety of materials such as plastic and steel.

Washington, D.C. and the Guggenheim Museum in New York City.

Born in Ciudad Bolívar in 1923, Soto studied in Caracas and Paris. His work is abstract, influenced by the Dutch painter Piet Mondrian and the American sculptor Alexander Calder. Many of Soto's pieces literally move, and he encourages viewers to see each piece from different perspectives.

Soto founded a museum in Ciudad Bolívar that exhibits his own work as well as works of other contemporary artists from South America, the United States, and Europe.

Other well-known Venezuelan painters and sculptors include Alejandro Colina, Francisco Narvaes, and Alejandro Otero. Colina created the famous statue in Caracas of María Lionza riding her tapir; works by Narvaes and Otero grace many outdoor spaces in Venezuela.

ARCHITECTURE

Primarily through the work of Carlos Raúl Villanueva, Venezuela has become a bastion of architectural art. Educated in Paris, Villanueva returned to Caracas to found the College of Architecture at the Central University of Caracas. He supervised the construction of a housing project in one of the poorest neighborhoods of Caracas. Finished in 1943, El Silencio, as the project is known, was the first low-cost housing project to be constructed in Latin America on such a large scale.

Although Villanueva went on to design other similar projects, his finest work is thought to be the University City in Caracas. He stylized the structural layout of the campus with plazas, patios, gardens, and canopied walkways, and he commissioned other artists, such as Alexander Calder, Jean Arp, and Fernand Léger, to create murals and sculptures to further embellish the university landscape.

Villanueva also designed the Olympic Stadium and Olympic Pool, the Museum of Fine Arts, and the Maestranza César Girón bull ring in Maracay.

Maternity **is the name of this sculpture by Lobo; it stands in front of a building designed by Carlos Raúl Villanueva.**

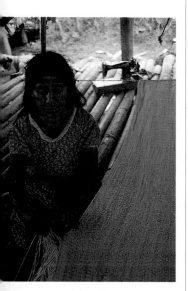

Above: **An Indian in the Orinoco Delta weaves hammocks for her family.**

Right: **A roadside stall in Mérida selling folk crafts.**

FOLK ARTS

Folk traditions in music, dance, and art have been of particular interest to Venezuelan youths since the early 1960s. Many traditional Venezuelan musical instruments that are played during holidays and religious festivals are Spanish in origin. The *cuatro* ("KWAH-troh"), or four-stringed guitar, which sounds a little like a ukulele, is often played along with the *maracas* ("mah-RAH-cahs"), while people dance the *joropo*, a rhythmic, fast step with many regional variations.

Other dances include the waltz, the merengue of Caribbean origin, and a version of the Argentine tango called the *tanguito* ("tahn-goo-WEE-toh"). Percussion instruments of African origin may accompany Spanish songs, such as *tono* ("TOH-noh") *llanero*, which is sung by the cowboys.

Indigenous Indians in Venezuela, especially the more isolated groups south of the Orinoco River, have a special chant for religious events. They also play a flute and a percussion instrument called a *culo en tierro* ("KOO-loh ehn tih-AIR-roh"), which is half a coconut husk placed face down on the ground and used as a drum.

Venezuela's indigenous Indians may weave colorful hammocks to sell at roadside stalls.

Indigenous Indian handicrafts are made either for personal use or for sale to tourists. The Guajiro Indians are especially well-known for their ceramics and their hammocks, which come in two varieties: a tight weave, or *hamaca*, and a loose weave, or *chinchorro*. Guajiro women create bright-colored designs on large looms at home. They also weave intricately patterned shawls and bags. Guajiro men are famous for their belts and saddlebags. Typical colors are yellow, red, and blue or green.

The Warau Indians of the Orinoco Delta are known not only for hammocks, but also for delicate baskets woven from dyed palm fibers and intricate wooden figurines carved in the shape of animals, insects, birds, fish, snakes, and dolphins.

Groups in the Amazonas Federal Territory, such as the Makiritare, Piaroa, and Yanomami, also make beautiful baskets, masks, blowpipes, feather and bead ornaments, rings from black stones, and carved hardwood stools. The mountain people of the Andes knit sweaters, woolen blankets, and ponchos called *ruanas* ("roo-AH-nahs"). *Llaneros* are known for rope-soled shoes, handmade leather goods such as lassos, and musical instruments such as the harp, *cuatro*, and *maracas*.

LEISURE

VENEZUELAN LEISURE TIME is spent playing sports, watching television, listening to the radio, reading the newspaper, or simply chatting with friends over coffee. There are also national parks for contact with nature, museums for educational recreation, golf courses for relaxing exercise, and theaters and nightclubs for entertainment.

Traditional Venezuelans spend a lot of their leisure time at home with their family, celebrating birthdays and religious holidays or simply getting together on weekends. For recreation, upper-class *caraqueños*, like urban North Americans, often go to shopping malls, to the movies, to cafés and restaurants, or to a private club.

In rural areas, it is at the local grocery store that people congregate to relax and discuss the events of the day.

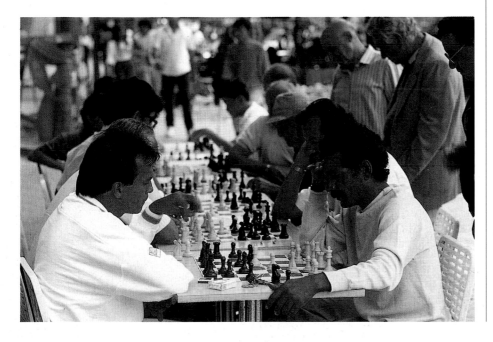

Left: **Both spectators and players enjoy chess in the outdoors in Caracas.**

Opposite: **Hikers in the Canaima National Park. Mountain ranges in the east, west, and south of the country present ample climbing opportunities.**

Venezuelan major leaguers Oswaldo (Ozzie) Guillén (*far right*) and Carlos Martinez began their careers with the La Guaira Sharks. Guillén played in the Chicago White Sox from 1985 to 1997; he is now with the Tampa Bay Devil Rays.

BASEBALL—THE NATIONAL SPORT

Baseball came to Venezuela from the United States in the 1890s. A group of upper-class Venezuelan students opened the first club in Caracas in 1895. Latin American countries that had the greatest enthusiasm for baseball—Cuba, Nicaragua, the Dominican Republic, Panama, Colombia, and Venezuela—felt a strong North American presence; countries where soccer predominated—Brazil, Argentina, Chile, Uruguay, and Peru—were more influenced by the Europeans.

The earliest Venezuelan baseball teams were made up of the sons of wealthy families living in an affluent suburb of Caracas called El Paraíso, where a baseball field was built in 1902. Soon, people from all walks of life formed street teams, and the sport gained mass appeal. After 1918, teams began to be organized more professionally, and by 1949, the government had instituted a program to build baseball fields and stadiums all over the country.

The professional baseball season in Venezuela lasts from October to February. Some well-known North American major leaguers play in Venezuela during their off-season, while Venezuelan major leaguers hit fields in the United States between March and September.

Venezuelans have played for the Toronto Blue Jays, the New York Yankees, the Chicago Cubs and White Sox, and the Cincinnati Reds, among others. Famous Venezuelan major leaguers include Luis Sojo, Omar Vizquel, and Andrés "Big Cat" Galarraga. Magglio Ordóñez is one of Venezuela's biggest new-generation baseball stars.

Venezuelan baseball teams include the Caracas Lions, the Magallanes Navigators, the Zulia Eagles, the Aragua Tigers, and the Lara Cardinals.

LESSER SPORTS

Soccer, basketball, and boxing are also popular in Venezuela, at both amateur and professional levels. Volleyball games, wrestling matches, and automobile and bicycle races are also usually well-attended.

In small towns, people enjoy watching and betting on cockfights. A lot of money is wagered on these well-trained birds, even though their competitive careers can be over in a matter of minutes.

Betting on racehorses is another popular leisure activity. The bet, called the *cinco y seis* ("SIN-koh ee SEYS"), a kind of daily double, has become so popular that the phrase is used to describe any unlikely possibility. The Rinconada Hippodrome in Caracas is one of the most sophisticated tracks in Latin America; it has 2,000 stables and even a swimming pool for horses. On weekends, 20,000 Venezuelans pack the grandstands to watch the races firsthand, while millions watch the races on television.

About 10 to 12 bullfights are held each year in Caracas, but most of the matadors come from abroad. Bullfights are also held in Maracay, Valencia, Mérida, and San Cristóbal. Rodeos, or *toros coleados* ("TOH-rohs coh-lay-AH-dos"), are held in small towns in the *llanos*.

Along the Caribbean coast, water sports such as deep-sea fishing, scuba diving, snorkeling, waterskiing, and sailing are quite popular.

Baseball is to Venezuelans what soccer is to the British; it is the national obsession. Nearly every town in Venezuela has its own stadium and team. Fans cheer with gusto for their favorite players. Some 200,000 boys aged 5 to 18 play in amateur leagues.

Telenovelas,
also known as
teleculebras, *or
television snakes,
are often stories
about the lives and
loves of a group of
not-too-likable
people. A show
called* Pasionaria
(Passionate) *was a
hit in Venezuela*.

OTHER AMUSEMENTS

For entertainment, Venezuelans in the cities often attend cultural performances such as the ballet and symphony; many also go to the movies. Although Venezuela has its own filmmaking industry, most of the films screened in the theaters are imported from Europe and the United States and dubbed in Spanish.

Watching television is a common diversion for Venezuelans of all social classes. Television came to the country in 1952. Now, there are six regular stations, three of which are government-owned. Most Venezuelans have regular access to television; there are more than four million television sets in use. Among the lower classes, the television set is a status symbol; it is not uncommon to see television antennas on the roofs of the *ranchos,* or shanties, that crowd the outskirts of the urban areas.

While Venezuela imports many television shows from the United States and other Latin American countries, it also provides news and entertainment in Spanish to Latin America, Spain, Portugal, and the growing Hispanic population in the United States. Venevision, the country's top television channel, reaches 8 million viewers around the world.

Soap operas, or *telenovelas* ("tay-lay-noh-BAY-lahs"), are extremely popular. Due to their adult content, they are broadcast at night, when children are asleep. Some Venezuelan *telenovelas* are exported to the United States for Latin American communities there.

Radio is also popular in Venezuela. In the late 1990s, there were 201 AM stations and 20 FM stations in Caracas and nearly 11 million radios in the country. The government owns eight stations that broadcast mostly cultural and educational programs.

In 1999, there were 11 Internet service providers in Venezuela and 27.8 personal computers to every 1,000 people.

The highest cable car station in the world, at 14,740 feet (4,493 m), is above Mérida in the Venezuelan Andes.

LEISURE AND SOCIAL LIFE

The private club is the center of social activities for the upper classes. On Sundays, upper-class families gather at the club to make use of the facilities: squash courts, swimming pools, restaurants, gyms, and spas. Some women also spend weekdays at the club with friends, either playing cards or having luncheons or tea parties. Men tend to gather at the club to drink, play dominoes or cards, or chat with friends.

In rural areas, men gather at the general store on Sundays and in the evenings to drink beer or sugarcane alcohol and occasionally play lawn bowling. Other customers who enter the store at these times usually make their purchases promptly and leave.

In very poor areas, social life is even more informal. People tend to chat with their neighbors while doing the household chores or sitting on the patio. More active socializing takes place during momentous occasions such as weddings, funerals, and religious festivals.

FESTIVALS

VENEZUELAN FESTIVALS, or fiestas, are usually religious, although some have political origins. All Venezuelans celebrate Christmas, Easter, and Independence Day, but some of the other holidays, such as patron saints' days are celebrated only in certain towns or villages. The same patron saint's day may be observed differently in different villages, although most celebrations include fireworks, processions, street dances, and games. Depending on the history of the town, festival customs can have an African, Spanish, or Indian flavor, or a blend of all three.

Festivals in Venezuela are often times for families to take a holiday. In the larger cities, holidays such as Holy Week—the week before Easter—have lost their religious significance and become occasions for families to go on a holiday. Many urban dwellers—and nearly all *caraqueños*—leave the city during Holy Week to travel abroad or to visit relatives in nearby states.

In many Andean towns, however, Holy Week is celebrated with great vigor: passion plays are acted out, robed and hooded repentants go to Mass on their knees, and large images of Judas are burned in the town square.

In many rural areas, religious festivals and patron saints' days provide the only real entertainment for farming families during the year. Festivities sponsored by local religious groups, merchants, or prominent citizens give people a chance to meet old friends and family members, watch cockfights, attend special Masses and elaborate processions, and dance, drink, and listen to music all night.

Above: **The celebration of Dia de San Pedro.**

Opposite: **Venezuelans celebrate Carnival, the colorful festival of indulgence that throws South America into joyful chaos before the fasting season of Lent.**

CALENDAR OF HOLIDAYS IN VENEZUELA

These are Venezuela's national holidays and festivals.

January 1	New Year's Day	July 5	Independence Day
February/March	Two days Carnival		(*below*, an artist's
	Ash Wednesday		impression of the first
March/April	Holy Thursday		Independence Day,
	Good Friday		in 1811)
	Easter	July 24	Birth of Simón Bolívar
April 19	Declaration of	October 12	Columbus Day
	Independence	November 1	All Saints' Day
May 1	Labor Day (often also	December 17	Death of Simón Bolívar
	Ascension and Corpus	December 24	Christmas Eve
	Christi Day)	December 25	Christmas Day
June 24	Battle of Carabobo	December 31	New Year's Eve

A carnival float in the coastal town of Carúpano.

CARNIVAL

In Caracas and some other towns, the principal fiesta is Carnival, a two-day celebration that takes place in either February or March on the Monday or Tuesday before Ash Wednesday. Carnival is the last festivity before the six-week period of Lent. Hence, people dress up in wild costumes, dance in the streets, and live a bit recklessly in anticipation of the weeks of personal sacrifice and religious contemplation that will follow. Most stores and businesses close during Carnival.

The festivities begin with a large parade, complete with elaborately decorated floats and people dressed in colorful costumes. Entire streets are roped off during the festival so people can dance the *joropo* and other Venezuelan dances and sing traditional songs.

In Caracas, water fights are common during Carnival, and people are known to decorate statues of Simón Bolívar with wreaths and flowers. In the town of El Callao in Bolívar State, calypso music of Caribbean origin is played, while in the German village of Colonia Tovar, a mock funeral is held to mark the end of the festivities.

Opposite: **The Devil Dancers of Yare during Corpus Christi.**

CORPUS CHRISTI

This is probably the most colorful festival in Venezuela. Celebrated on the Thursday after Trinity Sunday, it takes place about nine weeks after Easter in the town of San Francisco de Yare in Miranda State and in some villages in the states of Aragua and Carabobo.

Legend has it that a humble nun, Saint Juliana, often had visions while praying. One day, Christ appeared to her and indicated the meaning of her visions: the absence of a festival to honor the Blessed Sacrament. Thus, the Festival of Corpus Christi began in honor of the Eucharist—the bread and wine Catholics believe transform into the body and blood of Christ when consecrated during Mass.

For the famous festival that takes place in San Francisco de Yare, people dress up in baggy red costumes with crosses pinned to them, carry rosaries, and wear papier-mâché horned masks that resemble frightening bulls' heads. They are called the Devil Dancers.

At 6 A.M. on the morning of the festival, the dancers gather in front of the village church and dance vigorously to the beat of Venezuelan music. They attend Mass in the church and then return to their dancing, which by now has become even fiercer. Afterward, they visit the homes of important people in the village, who give them money or liquor.

In the afternoon, another procession forms near the church; each time it approaches the Devil Dancers, the members of the procession recoil in fear. Finally, all return to the church, where the Devil Dancers take off their masks and receive Holy Communion.

It is believed that the dancing and musical styles used during the celebration of Corpus Christi in San Francisco de Yare derive directly from non-Christian rituals practiced by the Ayoman Indians who used to inhabit the region.

CHRISTMAS IN VENEZUELA

The celebration of Christmas in Venezuela has undergone rather drastic changes in recent years. In the old days, people used to set up a *nacimiento* ("nah-sih-mih-EHN-toh"), or nativity scene, in the patio or living room of their home. The *nacimiento* contained small carved images of the holy family, the wise men, shepherds and sheep, stable animals, and a star. The background had houses, lakes, and roads, and the whole scene was placed on folded cloth resembling mountains.

Passers-by would admire the *nacimiento* through the windows of the living room, and the family would gather there in the evening to sing carols or recount the Christmas story. The figure of the baby Jesus was placed in the manger only on Christmas Eve, and the figures of the Three Kings were situated far from the child and moved up a little bit every day until they reached him on January 6, the Epiphany.

In the past, Venezuelan children did not know Santa Claus; they got their gifts from the Three Kings. And they opened their presents on Epiphany, rather than on Christmas. The children would place their shoes under their beds on the night of January 5, and in the morning, they would find their shoes filled with small toys, fruit, and other treats.

A *nacimiento*.

It was also a tradition to begin attending Christmas Mass as early as December 16, at 4 A.M.! After Mass, churchgoers would be met by groups singing carols and playing *maracas;* then they would drink the traditional after-Mass cup of sweetened black coffee and munch on a crispy corn fritter called a *masa* ("MAH-sah"), which could be purchased from a woman frying the fritters on a small grill by the road.

More recently, Venezuelans celebrating Christmas, especially young people, rollerskate in the village plaza all night long, indulge in hot chocolate and long fried doughnuts in the shape of twisted ropes, and then attend Mass at dawn.

These traditions still take place in some areas, but they are dying out. The typical Venezuelan Christmas is now much like the typical North American Christmas. Gifts from Santa Claus rather than the Three Kings are wrapped in festive paper and placed under the Christmas tree to be opened on Christmas morning.

The traditional *furruco* is still very much a part of Christmas celebrations in Venezuela.

One Venezuelan Christmas tradition that has not been lost, however, is the inclusion of music in the celebration. Young people train for months to compete in Christmas music competitions in which *gaitas* ("GAY-tahs"), or bands playing traditional Venezuelan instruments, attempt to outperform one another. *Gaita* instruments usually consist of a four-stringed guitar, or *cuatro*, a common drum, *maracas*, and an unusual percussion instrument called a *furruco* ("foo-ROO-koh"). This is a drum with a hole in the center into which a long stick is inserted and rubbed up and down to create a hoarse, resonant sound.

Gaitas move from house to house at Christmas, especially in Caracas, playing traditional music and accompanied by choruses singing Venezuelan songs.

PATRON SAINTS' DAYS

Nearly every Venezuelan village has a patron saint and an annual festival held in the saint's honor. It is customary to carry images of the patron saint through the streets in formal procession, after which dances, bullfights, competitions, and rodeos take center stage.

East of Caracas, in the village of Guatire, celebrants honor Saint Peter by blackening their faces and donning top hats. Saint Peter used to be invoked throughout the Christian world against fever because, according to the Bible, Christ cured Saint Peter's mother-in-law of a fever. Legend in Guatire has it that a slave woman's child was cured through her prayers to Saint Peter, and she danced all day to offer her thanks to the saint. Saint Peter's Day is thus celebrated with dancing somewhat resembling that of the Devil Dancers on Corpus Christi.

The festival of Saint John is celebrated primarily on the Caribbean coast in Miranda State, which has a large African population. This festival has elements that are distinctly African in origin. The framework of the fiesta is Spanish, but the music that accompanies the dancing is played on African drums. The festival is associated with the summer festivals of pre-Christian times, where fires were lit to greet the beginning of summer, and celebrants gathered round and jumped through the fires and sang traditional songs praising both saint and season. Taking place from June 23 through June 25, the festival of Saint John is remarkable for its unrelenting street dancing.

The festival of Saint Benito, or Saint Benedict, on December 27 also has a strong African heritage, although it is now celebrated by Venezuelans of all ethnic groups. In the area near Lake Maracaibo, St. Benito is honored differently from village to village. The Paruajano Indians of Sinamaica Lagoon place images of the saint in boats and sail to a designated area

The celebration of Dia de San Benito in Santo Domingo.

where a special altar has been erected to honor him. Then, the drumming starts and the villagers take turns dancing with images of the saint. In El Mojan, which is very close to the lagoon, *criollo* celebrants carry saint figures through the streets, dancing an entirely different step to the music of the *cuatro* and different drums.

In Gibraltar and Bobures, African people celebrate with yet another form of dancing that is distinctly African in tempo. In Timotes, in Mérida state, dancers carry *maracas*, blacken their faces with paint, and wear black grass skirts and feathered headdresses. Others don the traditional Venezuelan *liquiliqui* or wear a cowboy-like costume with a red fringe.

FOOD

THE CUISINE OF VENEZUELA—like its customs and traditions, religious rituals, and language—shows Indian, Spanish, and African influences. Many staples of the Venezuelan diet were cultivated by the Indians in precolonial days, and many ingredients commonly used in local dishes originally came from Spain and Africa during the colonial period.

The early Indians of South America cultivated corn, beans, and squash. Upon their arrival in the New World, the Spanish *conquistadores* found other foods such as avocados, Brazil nuts, chocolate, guavas, manioc (bitter cassava), papayas, passion fruit, pineapples, and tomatoes.

While the *conquistadores* brought many of these foods back to Spain, they also brought chickens, pigs, garlic, onions, olive oil, rice, *garbanzo* ("gar-BAHN-zoh") beans, or chickpeas, and sugarcane to South America. Two Spanish-derived dishes are Spanish omelette—chickpea flour batter over boiled potato slices and broccoli florets—and Spanish rice—white rice fried with onions, red peppers, carrots, and other vegetables.

Coffee, the most beloved drink of South America, originated in Ethiopia and made its way to South America via the Middle East. Bananas and plantains, which are very much a part of the Venezuelan diet, came to the New World from Africa and the Canary Islands, although they originated in India and Malaysia.

Many of the ingredients brought from the outside world were readily accepted into the Venezuelan diet. Over the years, they were adapted to suit the *criollo* palate, and what emerged was a cuisine that, while sharing some cooking traditions with other Latin American cultures, was in many ways unique to Venezuela. This cuisine, called *comida criolla*, is based essentially on pancakes, soups and stews, and meats such as chicken, pork, and beef. Cheap set meals served in some restaurants in Venezuela usually include a soup with the main course.

Opposite: **Reaching for an** *empanada*, **a deep-fried turnover.**

Cachapas—sweet corn pancakes served with cheese—toast on a griddle, ready to be sold at this roadside stall.

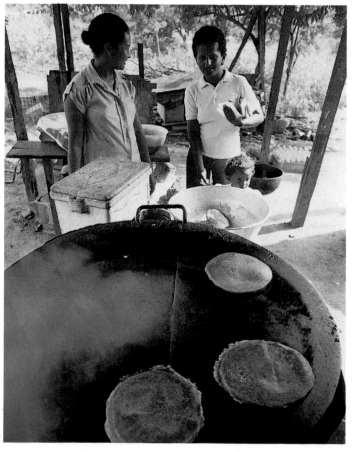

SPECIALTIES

AREPA ("ah-RAY-pah") Of Indian origin, this staple of the Venezuelan diet resembles a very thick Mexican tortilla. It is made by mixing either yellow or white corn flour with salt and enough water to make a dough. After being formed into a ball or patty, the *arepa* is toasted on a griddle, wrapped in a napkin, and served in a straw basket. To enhance its flavor, the *arepa* may be stuffed with ground beef, cheese, avocado, tuna, ham, eggs, beans, shrimp, and even shark. Eaten on its own, the *arepa* is almost tasteless; the stuffed *arepas*, however, are delicious.

Caraqueños often eat *arepas* in restaurants called *areperas* ("ah-ray-PAIR-rahs") rather than at home, although prepared *arepa* flour is available in grocery stores.

BLACK BEANS Black beans are a popular item on the Venezuelan menu across economic and social classes. The main ingredients in the national dish, *pabellon* ("pah-beh-YON") *criollo*, are stewed shredded meat, rice, and black beans, topped with sautéed bananas. *Pabellon criollo* is based on a 16th-century Spanish recipe called *ropa vieja* ("ROH-pah bih-EH-hah"), which means old clothes. Many Venezuelans say that no restaurant could possibly prepare good *pabellon criollo*; this dish has to be prepared at home, according to secret family recipes.

SOPA DE FRIJOLES NEGROS (BLACK BEAN SOUP)

This recipe makes soup for six.

1 pound (454 g) black beans
1 chopped medium onion
2 cloves garlic, chopped
½ teaspoon cumin
1 teaspoon hot red chili, dried and crumbled
6 cups (1.4 l) beef stock
Salt to taste
1 chopped hard-boiled egg (optional)

Rinse the beans and soak them overnight. When ready to cook, drain the beans and rinse again. Place the beans in a large saucepan. Add the beef stock, chopped onion and garlic, cumin, and chili. Cover and simmer over low heat for about 2 ½ hours, until the beans are very soft. (The time will vary, depending on the age of the beans.) Puree the beans in a food processor, adding some of the beef stock. (Puree in batches, if necessary.) Pour the puree into the saucepan. Season with salt and heat through. Serve garnished with chopped hard-boiled egg, if liked.

Aside from the home favorites, Caracas and major cities in Venezuela have a wide variety of ethnic restaurants that serve Arab, Chinese, Japanese, Hungarian, Portuguese, Colombian, Mexican, Trinidadian, Cuban, Swiss, and German food.

HALLACA A dish that unifies the national cuisine is the *hallaca* ("ah-YAH-kah"). Traditionally made at Christmas, the *hallaca* is the dish that Venezuelans yearn for when they are away from home. They say one can cook the *hallaca* properly only after years of practice and with the help of the whole family. Invented by the Indians in precolonial days, *hallacas* are essentially little corn dough pies filled with meat, chicken, or other ingredients, wrapped inside a banana leaf in a flat rectangle, and boiled. The banana leaf seals in and enhances the flavor of the *hallaca*. Different regions add their own special touches: eggs, olives, raisins, or vegetables. But, no matter what the ingredients, a platter of *hallacas* occupies the seat of honor on the Christmas Eve dining table.

Cooking a traditional meal in a modern kitchen in Caracas.

DESSERTS

Several Venezuelan dishes are made using coconut or coconut milk: rice dishes, meat stews and soups, and especially desserts. A famous Venezuelan cake, *bien me sabe de coco* ("bih-ehn may SAH-bay day KOH-koh"), is made by moistening plain cake with muscatel wine and coconut cream. Coconut is also used in candies or combined with caramel to make what is called a *coquito* ("koh-KIH-toh").

Flan, a type of Spanish pudding of baked egg custard with a caramel topping, is also served for dessert as are a wide variety of tropical fruits such as mango, guava, pineapple, and papaya.

COFFEE

South Americans are great coffee drinkers. They drink a cup at each meal and several times in between meals. Friends often meet each other in the street and go to a café or a little outdoor coffee stand to indulge in a cup of coffee and some satisfying gossip.

Although about half the world's coffee is now grown in Latin America, the plant itself originally came from Africa. From there, it traveled to the Arab nations where it became an acceptable stimulant for Muslims, who are forbidden to drink alcohol. Coffee arrived in Europe with the Turkish invaders in the early 1600s, and in Latin America in the 1720s. Brazil and Colombia are famous for their excellent coffee, and the Venezuelan crop, though small, is reasonably good. In fact, Venezuela produces the famous *café azul de Caracas* ("KAH-fay ah-ZOOL day kah-RAH-kass"), or the blue coffee bean of Caracas, which is of very high quality.

Coffee is so popular in Venezuela that the drink has a vocabulary of its own: *café con leche* ("KAH-fay kon LEH-chay") is coffee with hot milk; a large cup of mild black coffee is called a *guayoyo* ("goo-ay-YOH-yoh"); a *negro* ("NAY-groh") is a large cup of strong black coffee; a *negrito* ("nay-GRIH-toh") is a small cup or demitasse of strong black coffee; a *cafecito* ("kah-fay-SIH-toh") is a demitasse of sweetened coffee; a large cup of strong coffee with a little milk added is called a *marron* ("mah-ROHN"); and a demitasse of strong coffee with a little milk added is called a *marroncito* ("mah-rahn-SIH-toh").

Coffee knows no class barriers in South America; it is enjoyed by both subsistence farmer and wealthy entrepreneur.

127

EATING OUT

Caraqueños eat out regularly and often. Whether they opt for a pizza parlor, a fast-food outlet, or a famous French restaurant in an elegant hotel, *caraqueños* have a wide variety of places to eat at. The most popular places include *criollo* restaurants specializing in local cuisine, pasta places, *areperas* that often open all night, steak houses specializing in Argentine cuisine, and Spanish restaurants where *tascas* ("TAHS-cahs"), or grilled seafood snacks, are offered and dining is accompanied by Spanish music.

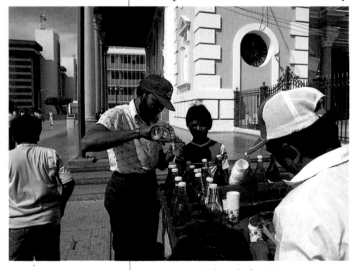

A soft drinks stall in Maracaibo. Many people find work selling food and drink on the streets.

Restaurateurs use ingredients that are grown only in Venezuela for some recipes: rice from Guárico State, tomatoes and miniature peppers from Margarita Island, freshwater prawns and lobsters from the Caribbean, beef from the *llanos*. After dinner, many young people like to spend time in piano bars or cafés, enjoying coffee, fresh fruit shakes, and dessert.

Caracas has the most sophisticated international cuisine, but many states have famous dishes of their own: Zulia is known for fish from Lake Maracaibo and plantains; Trujillo for pastries and braised chicken; Mérida for dishes made from local chickpeas and green peas; Falcón for goat's meat recipes and cheese and fudge made from goat's milk; Bolívar for fish stews; the Caribbean states for an array of fresh seafood dishes including *pargo* ("PAR-goh"), or red snapper; and Táchira for chicken soup made with milk and hot peppers.

EATING AT HOME

The typical Caracas family wakes up for breakfast at 6 A.M. so the children can be in school by 7 A.M. Standard breakfast fare includes eggs, *arepas*, bread or rolls, fresh fruit juice, and coffee. Lunch is served from noon to 2 P.M. and is the most important meal of the day. A typical lunch consists of soup, salad, meat and vegetables, fruit, and dessert, which is often a pastry or tart. Water, soft drinks, beer, or lemonade washes down the meal.

Dinner is usually a light meal, and it is served late, at about 9 P.M. *Arepas*, soup, and a sandwich or eggs are typical dinner fare. Some Venezuelans have hot chocolate before bed or at breakfast. Men drink whiskey, beer, rum, or wine at the cocktail hour; women rarely consume alcohol.

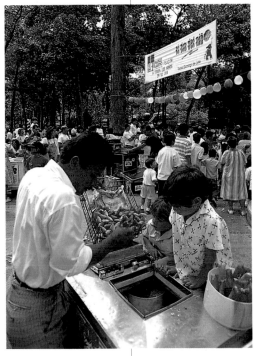

Attractive colors attract children to a vendor at a fair.

Although lunch is the most significant meal of the day for families in Venezuela, dinner is the meal most associated with entertaining. Some dinner parties begin as late as 11 P.M., and do not end until 3 A.M. or later. Even if a dinner begins early, it can end as late as midnight. The wife and husband usually sit at the head and foot of the table, with the guest of honor next to one or the other.

At upper-class gatherings, the food is served by a maid, and guests are not permitted to start eating until everyone at table has been served. When hosting a dinner party, Venezuelans do not push their guests to finish everything on their plates or to have additional helpings. When guests have had their fill, they often place the knife and fork together, pointing at ten o'clock.

CAVIAR CRILLO (NATIVE CAVIAR)

1 cup (237 ml) dried black beans
1 coarsely chopped large onion
5 tablespoons olive oil
3 cloves garlic, pressed

6 red chilies, seeded and crushed
2 teaspoons crushed cumin seeds
Salt to taste

Cook the beans in slightly salted water for about an hour until they are tender. Drain the beans and set aside. Sauté the chopped onion in two tablespoons of olive oil until it is soft. Add the garlic, chilies, and cumin. Continue to cook for two minutes. Add the beans and remaining olive oil. Add salt to taste. Mix well.

AREPA (CORN CAKES)

This recipe makes five *arepas*.

2 cups (473 ml) water
2 teaspoons salt
1 teaspoon cooking oil

2 cups (473 ml) finely ground, pre-cooked, corn meal (preferably white)
Butter and cheese (optional)

Pour the water into a large bowl and add the salt and cooking oil. Slowly add the corn meal, and kneed into a dough. (Cheese may be mixed in to add flavor to the dough.) Pat a small amount of the dough into a flat, round cake about ¼ inch (roughly 6 mm) thick. Smooth the edges of the cake. Make as many cakes as needed to use up the dough. Heat a greased skillet or griddle over a low flame. Place the cakes on the griddle, a few at a time, to brown on both sides. Then place

them in the oven to bake for about 15 minutes. To serve, slice each *arepa* as you would a hamburger bun, remove a little of the soft steaming meal from the middle, stuff with desired filling, and close the *arepa*. Alternatively, make the *arepas* about the size of a dollar coin and fry in oil until golden brown on both sides. Serve as a bread with butter and cheese.

ARROZ CON LECHE (RICE WITH MILK)

12 tablespoons rice
1 cup (237 ml) water
4 cups (1 l) milk
6 tablespoons sugar
1 cinnamon stick
Powdered cinnamon
   (optional)

Wash rice thoroughly and place in water over a hot stove. When water has evaporated, add milk and cinnamon stick. Cook over low heat to a creamy consistency. Add sugar and salt. Cook until thick, constantly stirring.

Remove from fire. When a little cooler, sprinkle powdered cinnamon.

ROPA VIEJA AL ESTILO VENEZOLANO (SHREDDED BEEF)

This recipe serves six.

2 pounds (907 g) flank steak in one piece
2 cups (437 ml) beef stock
3 tablespoons corn oil
1 chopped onion
2 cloves garlic, chopped

2 sweet red peppers, seeded and chopped
¼ teaspoon cumin
1 teaspoon hot paprika or hot sauce
Salt
Freshly ground pepper

Place the beef into a flameproof casserole and pour in enough stock to cover it. Bring to a simmer, cover and cook over low heat until it is tender, about 2 hours. Cool in the stock. Remove the beef and shred it. Cover and set aside. Reserve the stock. Heat the oil in a large frying pan and sauté the onion, garlic and red peppers until they are soft. Add the tomatoes, cumin, paprika, salt and pepper and cook for 5 minutes longer, until the mixture is thick and well blended. Stir in the reserved shredded beef and about half a cup of the stock and simmer for 5 minutes longer to blend the flavors. Taste for seasoning and add more hot paprika, if liked. Serve with rice.

N

CARIBBEAN SEA

Paraguaná Peninsula

Punto Fijo ●
● Coro
FALCÓN
Gulf of Venezuela

San Rafael ●
Maracaibo ●
San Francisco ●
● Cabimas

DISTRITO FEDERAL

NUEVA ESPARTA
Tortuga Is.
Margarita Is.
● La Asunción

TRINIDAD AND TOBAGO

YARACUY
LARA
Barquisimeto ●
Ciudad Ojeda ●
Maracaibo Lake
ZULIA

Puerto Cabello ●
Valencia ●
CARABOBO
● Maracay
MIRANDA
CARACAS

Carúpano ●
Cumaná ●
SUCRE
● Port of Spain

TRUJILLO
Valera ● Trujillo
MERIDA
Mérida ▲ *Pico Bolívar (16,427 ft.)*

San Carlos ●
COJEDES
ARAGUA

Barcelona ●

Anaco ●
MONAGAS

Tucupita ●

PORTUGUESA
Guanare ●
● Barinas
BARINAS

Calabozo ●
GUÁRICO
Valle de la Pascua ●

El Tigre ●
ANZOÁTEGUI

Curiapo ●
DELTA AMACURO

TÁCHIRA
San Cristóbal ●

San Fernando de Apure ●

Ciudad Guayana ●

Ciudad Bolívar ●

Elorza ●
APURE

El Dorado ●

Poci ●
GUYANA

Puerto Páez ●
Meta
Orinoco
Apure
Paragua
Caura
BOLÍVAR
Angel Falls (3,212 ft.)
Caroni
Mt. Roraima ▲ *(2,810 ft.)*

COLOMBIA

Puerto Ayacucho ●

San Fernando de Atabapo ●
AMAZONAS
Orinoco
Casiquiare

BRAZIL

Legend:
● Capital city
● Major town
▲ Mountain peak

Height of land (feet)
over 9,000
6,000 – 9,000
3,000 – 6,000
1,500 – 3,000
600 – 1,500
0 – 600

A   B   C   D

1

2

3

4

5

MAP OF VENEZUELA

ECONOMIC VENEZUELA

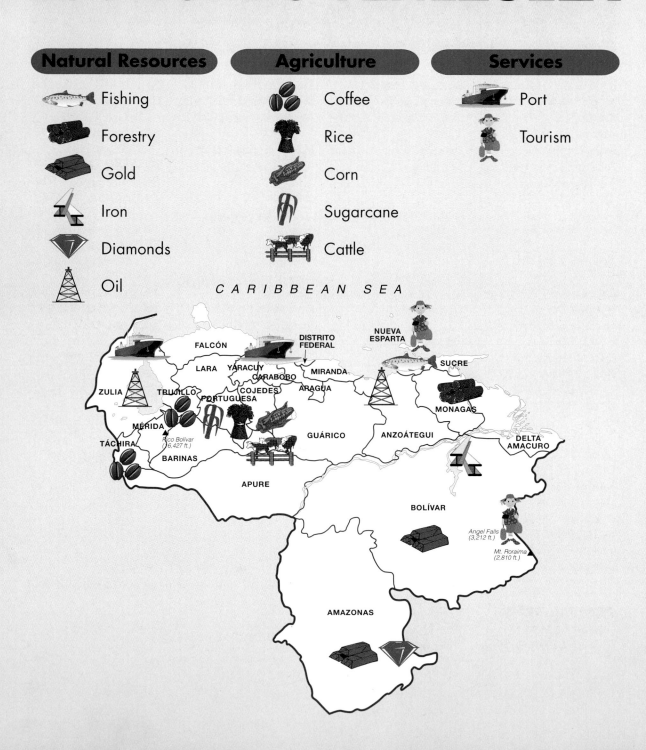

Natural Resources
- Fishing
- Forestry
- Gold
- Iron
- Diamonds
- Oil

Agriculture
- Coffee
- Rice
- Corn
- Sugarcane
- Cattle

Services
- Port
- Tourism

CARIBBEAN SEA

FALCÓN

DISTRITO FEDERAL

NUEVA ESPARTA

LARA YARACUY

CARABOBO MIRANDA

SUCRE

ZULIA

TRUJILLO COJEDES ARAGUA

PORTUGUESA

MONAGAS

MÉRIDA

Pico Bolívar
(16,427 ft.)

GUÁRICO

ANZOÁTEGUI

DELTA AMACURO

TÁCHIRA

BARINAS

APURE

BOLÍVAR

Angel Falls
(3,212 ft.)

Mt. Roraima
(2,810 ft.)

AMAZONAS

ABOUT THE ECONOMY

OVERVIEW
Petroleum dominates the Venezuelan economy, accounting for more than 60 percent of the GDP and around 80 percent of export earnings.

INDUSTRIES
Petroleum, mining, food processing, textiles, aluminum, steel, and motor vehicle assembly

GROSS DOMESTIC PRODUCT (GDP)
US$182.8 billion (1999)

GDP PER CAPITA
US$8,000 (1999)

GDP COMPOSITION
Industry 63 percent, services 33 percent, and agriculture 4 percent (1997)

GDP GROWTH
-7.2 percent (1999)

EXTERNAL DEBT
US$32 billion (1999)

CURRENCY
1 bolivar (Bs) = 100 centimos
US$1 = 652.33 Bs (January 2000)

INFLATION RATE
20 percent (1999)

AGRICULTURAL PRODUCTS
Corn, sorghum, sugarcane, rice, coffee, bananas, and vegetables

MAIN EXPORTS
Petroleum, bauxite, aluminum, steel, chemicals, and agricultural products

MAIN EXPORT PARTNERS
United States and Puerto Rico, Colombia, Brazil, Japan, Germany, Netherlands, Italy (1999)

MAIN IMPORTS
Raw materials, machinery and equipment, transportation equipment, and construction materials

MAIN IMPORT PARTNERS
United States, Japan, Colombia, Italy, Germany, France, Brazil, and Canada (1999)

LABOR FORCE
9.9 million (1999)

LABOR FORCE BY OCCUPATION
Services 64 percent, agriculture 23 percent, and industry 13 percent

UNEMPLOYMENT RATE
18 percent (1999)

CULTURAL VENEZUELA

La Zona Colonial de Coro
Coro's colonial center was declared a national monument in 1950. Its cobblestone streets and old colonial houses reflect the eminent role of the Spanish in Venezuela's history.

Garden City
Tree-filled Maracay is the "garden city of Venezuela." It also boasts a 7,000-seat bull ring and entry to the Henri Pittier National Park, 107,800 hectares (1,078 square km) of reserved land hosting some 550 bird species among other wildlife.

Colonia Tovar
Venezuela's gem of Germany is a little mountain town near the capital. Founded in 1843 as a settlement of German immigrants, Colonia Tovar is now a tourist spot offering Venezuelan and international visitors alike a glimpse of German culture.

Devil dance
This ceremony takes place in San Fransisco de Yare every Corpus Christi. Dancers put on papier-mache masks and red costumes and dance through the streets to the rhythm of drums and chants to scare off the devil.

Puerto La Cruz
Beautiful beaches, access to the Mochima National Park, and boats to Margarita Island and other neighboring islands are some of the major attractions of Barcelona.

Water sports
Tourists visit Margarita Island for snorkeling or scuba diving or just to lie on the sands of El Agua, the island's best beach. Other attractions include lagoons, cranes, three national parks, and the nearby fishing village of Pampatar, with its small colonial fort and colorful old

La Virgen de la Paz
A statue of the Virgin of Peace 153.2 feet (46.7 m) tall and weighing 2,000 pounds (907 kg) looks over the city of Trujillo from a mile above (1.6 km). Visitors can climb inside the monument to reach one of four points from which to see the city.

Map labels: FALCÓN, DISTRITO FEDERAL, NUEVA ESPARTA, LARA, YARACUY, CARACAS, SUCRE, ZULIA, CARABOBO, MIRANDA, ARAGUA, MONAGAS, TRUJILLO, COJEDES, MÉRIDA, PORTUGUESA, GUÁRICO, ANZOÁTEGUI, DELTA AMACURO, TÁCHIRA, BARINAS, Pico Bolívar (16,427 ft.), APURE, BOLÍVAR, Angel Falls (3,212 ft.), Mt. Roraima (2,810 ft.), AMAZONAS

Castillo de San Antonio
South America's oldest Spanish castle, the San Antonio castle, was restored after an earthquake in 1929. It now offers visitors a panoramic view of Cumaná's cobblestone streets, castles, fortresses, and museums.

Puerto Ayacucho
This tropical rain forest settlement was a camp set up in 1924 for workers building the highway to Samariapo which skirts the Orinoco upstream of Ayacucho. Indigenous Indians now come here to sell their handicrafts to tourists.

Bolivar Museum
Formerly the house where the country's first newspaper was published, now a museum exhibiting contemporary Venezuelan artworks as well as pre-Columbian art and some petroglyphs.

Jesús Soto Contemporary Art Museum
This museum in Ciudad Bolívar has eight rooms and several inner gardens exhibiting works by more than 130 artists from around the world, in particular the groundbreaking creations of Venezuelan kinetic artist Jesús Soto.

Mount Roraima
For nearly half a century, explorers could not find a way up this mile-high (1.6-km-high) sandstone plateau. Today, a single trail amid ancient forests and waterfalls leads hikers to the summit.

Canaima National Park
Canaima, meaning "God of Thunder," is 3 million hectares (million square km) of jungle containing the Gran Sabana and the world's highest waterfall, Angel Falls, which plunges 3,210 feet (980 m) from the Auyan Tepui, or "Devil Mountain."

ABOUT THE CULTURE

OFFICIAL NAME
Bolivarian Republic of Venezuela

FLAG DESCRIPTION
A red band at the bottom and a yellow band at the top sandwich a blue band containing an arc of seven white stars.

NATIONAL ANTHEM
Glorto al Bravo Pueblo que el Yugo Lanzo, or "Glory to the Brave Nation that Shook off the Yoke"

POPULATION
23,542,649 (July 2000)

AGE STRUCTURE
14 years and below: 33 percent
15 to 64 years: 63 percent
65 years and over: 4 percent

LIFE EXPECTANCY
Total population: 73 years
Men: 70 years; women: 76 years (2000 est.)

ETHNIC GROUPS
Spanish, Italian, Portuguese, Arab, German, African, and indigenous

MAIN RELIGIONS
Roman Catholic 96 percent, Protestant 2 percent

MAJOR LANGUAGES
Spanish (official), numerous indigenous dialects

LITERACY
91.1 percent of population aged 15 and above

NATIONAL HOLIDAYS
Declaration of Independence—April 19
Battle of Carabobo—June 24
Independence Day—July 5
Simón Bolívar's Birthday—July 24
Columbus Day—October 12
Death of Simón Bolívar—December 17

LEADERS IN POLITICS
Simón Bolívar (1783–1830)—revolutionary leader in the fight for independence
Rómulo Betancourt (1908–81)—leader of Acción Democrática and president 1945–48, 1959–64
Hugo Chávez Frías—president since 1998

LEADERS IN ARTS
Arturo Michelena—one of South America's best-known painters
Arturo Uslar Pietri—one of Venezuela's most celebrated authors
Jesús Soto—leader in kinetic art
Martin Tovar y Tovar—renowned muralist who painted the Battle of Carabobo on the ceiling of the national capital congress building
Rómulo Gallegos—author of Venezuela's most famous novel, *Dona Barbara*

TIME LINE

IN VENEZUELA	IN THE WORLD

5000–1500 B.C.
Mesoindian cultures
1000–1500 B.C.
Neoindian cultures
1500 B.C.
Indohispanic cultures

753 B.C.
Rome is founded.
116–17 B.C.
Roman Empire reaches its greatest extent, under
Emperor Trajan (98–17 B.C.).
A.D. 600
Height of Mayan civilization
1000
Chinese perfect gunpowder and begin to use it in
warfare.

1498
Columbus lands on the Paria Peninsula and
sees "the most beautiful lands in the world."
1515
Cumaná, Venezuela's first
colonial city, is founded.
1527
(Santa Ana de) Coro, an important city in
Venezuela's early history, is founded.

1530
Beginning of trans-Atlantic slave trade organized
by Portuguese in Africa
1558–1603
Reign of Elizabeth I of England
1620
Pilgrim Fathers sail the Mayflower to America.
1776
U. S. Declaration of Independence
1789–1799
The French Revolution

1806
Francisco de Miranda twice tries unsuccessfully
to liberate Venezuela from Spanish rule.
1811
The first national congress is formed
and issues a Declaration of Independence;
the first constitution is established.
1812
The First Republic falls as Monteverde
takes Caracas for Spain.
1813
Simón Bolívar establishes the Second Republic
and is proclaimed Liberator.

IN VENEZUELA	IN THE WORLD
1814	
Llanero leader José Tomás Boves captures Caracas, ending the Second Republic and re-establishing Spanish rule.	
1819	
Bolívar is proclaimed provisional president by a second congress; a second constitution is drafted.	
1821	
The Battle of Carabobo; Bolívar forms Gran Colombia.	
1829	
Venezuela leaves Gran Colombia.	
1835	
Dr. José María Vargas becomes Venezuela's first civilian president.	
	1861
	U.S. Civil War begins.
	1869
1878	The Suez Canal is opened.
The Bolívar becomes the currency; the national anthem is written.	
1908	
Juan Vicente Gómez begins his dictatorship.	**1914**
1935	World War I begins.
Eleazar López Contreras becomes president and eventually restores some of the democracy lost under Gómez.	**1939**
	World War II begins.
	1945
	The United States drops atomic bombs on Hiroshima and Nagasaki.
	1949
	North Atlantic Treaty Organization (NATO) formed
	1957
	Russians launch Sputnik.
	1966–1969
	Chinese Cultural Revolution
1973	
Carlos Andrés Pérez becomes president on a promise to tackle privilege and poverty issues. Venezuela becomes wealthy on an oil boom.	**1986**
	Nuclear power disaster at Chernobyl in Ukraine
	1991
	Break-up of Soviet Union
	1997
1999	Hong Kong is returned to China.
Hugo Chávez Frías comes to power; he promises to support the people and wage war against corruption.	**2001**
	World population surpasses 6 billion.

GLOSSARY

abrazo ("ah-BRAH-soh")
An embrace between Venezuelans when they meet.

caraqueño ("kah-rah-KAIR-nyoh")
A resident of Caracas.

comadre ("kom-MAH-dray")
Godmother.

compadre ("kom-PAH-dray")
Godfather.

criollo ("kree-OH-loh")
A Creole. Originally referred to a person of Spanish ancestry; now describes anyone or anything indigenous to Venezuela.

cuatro ("KWAH-troh")
A small guitar with four strings.

hacienda ("ah-sih-EHN-dah")
A large plantation or estate.

hamaca ("ah-MAH-kah")
A tightly-woven hammock.

llanero ("yah-NAIR-roh")
Someone who dwells in the *llanos*, usually a cowboy.

llanos ("YAH-noss")
The vast central plains of Venezuela.

manta ("MAHN-tah")
An intricately woven shawl worn by Spanish and Latin American women.

mestizo ("mehs-TEE-soh")
Originally referred to a person of mixed Spanish-Indian ancestry; now describes anyone of mixed ethnicity.

piñata ("pih-NYAH-tah")
Bright-colored animal figure filled with candy and toys; it is hit with a stick at children's birthday parties until it releases its contents.

quinceañera ("kin-seh-ah-nih-AIR-rah")
A girl's 15th birthday.

rancho ("RAHN-choh")
A makeshift home built on the outskirts of the large cities, especially around Caracas.

tepui ("tair-POO-ee")
A flat-topped rock formation in the Guiana Highlands.

Venezolano ("beh-neh-zoh-LAH-noh")
A Venezuelan.

FURTHER INFORMATION

Books

Boehm, Lincoln A. *Venezuela in Pictures*. Visual Geography series. Minneapolis: Lerner Publications Company, 1998.

Boulais, Sue. *Andres Galarraga: A Real-Life Reader Biography*. Elkton: Mitchell Lane Pub, 1998.

George, Jean Craighead. *One Day in the Tropical Rain Forest*. New York: Ty Crowell Company, 1990.

Heinrichs, Ann. *Venezuela*. San Francisco: Children's Press, 1994.

Horenstein, Henry. *Baseball in the Barrios*. San Diego: Gulliver Books, 1997.

Jones, Helga. *Venezuela*. Globe-Trotters Club series. Minneapolis: Carolrhoda Books, 2000.

———. *Venezuela*. A Ticket To series. Minneapolis: Carolrhoda Books, 2000.

Morrison, Marion. *Venezuela*. Major World Nations series. New York: Chelsea House Publishers, 1998.

Rawlins, Carol B. *The Orinoco River*. Watts Library: World of Water series. New York: Franklin Watts, 1999.

Websites

About the Auyantepui in the Roraima group of mountains. Includes a slide show. Http://www.mother.com/-cwitham/tepui.html#angelfalls

Country study of Venezuela. Http://www.lcweb2.loc.gov/frd/cs/vetoc.html

Embassy of Venezuela in the United States. Http://www.embavenez-us.org/

History of the Bolívar Peninsula and the life of Simón Bolívar. Http://www.crystalbeach.com/history.htm

Photos of and facts on the spectacled bear. Http://scz.org/animals/b/spbear.html

Virtual tour of Venezuela. Http://www.orinoco.org/

CDs

Folk Music from Venezuela. United Kingdom: Arc, 2000.

BIBLIOGRAPHY

Baguley, Kitt. *Culture Shock! Venezuela*. Singapore: Times Books International, 1999.

Country Report: Venezuela. London: Economist Intelligence Unit, 1993.

Devine, Elizabeth and Nancy L. Braganti. *The Travelers' Guide to Latin American Customs and Manners*. New York: St. Martin's Press, 1988.

Fodor's South America. New York and London: Fodor's Travel Publications, 1989.

Popic, Miro, ed. *Ecotourism Guide to Venezuela*. Caracas: Miro Popic, 2000.

South America, Central America & the Caribbean. London: Europa Publications, 1992.

Venezuela in Pictures. Minneapolis: Lerner Publications Company, 1987.

Amazon Watch. Http://www.amazonwatch.org

Facts about Venezuela. Http://www.latinsynergy.org

Think Venezuela. Http://www.think-venezuela.net

INDEX